The Reflexive Method Applied to the Problem of God in Lachelier and Lagneau

Series Board

James Bernauer

Drucilla Cornell

Thomas R. Flynn

Kevin Hart

Richard Kearney

Jean-Luc Marion

Adriaan Peperzak

Thomas Sheehan

Hent de Vries

Merold Westphal

Michael Zimmerman

John D. Caputo, *series editor*

Perspectives in
Continental
Philosophy

PAUL RICOEUR

The Reflexive Method Applied to the Problem of God in Lachelier and Lagneau

PREFACE BY JEAN GREISCH
TRANSLATED BY DAVID PELLAUER

FORDHAM UNIVERSITY PRESS
New York ■ *2026*

Copyright © 2026 Fordham University Press

This book was first published in French as *Méthode réflexive appliquée au problème de Dieu chez Lachelier et Lagneau*, by Paul Ricoeur © Les Éditions du Cerf, 2017.

All rights reserved. No part of this publication may be reproduced, stored in a retrieval system, or transmitted in any form or by any means—electronic, mechanical, photocopy, recording, or any other—except for brief quotations in printed reviews, without the prior permission of the publisher.

Fordham University Press has no responsibility for the persistence or accuracy of URLs for external or third-party Internet websites referred to in this publication and does not guarantee that any content on such websites is, or will remain, accurate or appropriate.

Fordham University Press also publishes its books in a variety of electronic formats. Some content that appears in print may not be available in electronic books.

Visit us online at www.fordhampress.com.

For EU safety / GPSR concerns: Mare Nostrum Group B.V., Mauritskade 21D, 1091 GC Amsterdam, The Netherlands, gpsr@mare-nostrum.co.uk.

Library of Congress Cataloging-in-Publication Data available online at https://catalog.loc.gov.

Printed in the United States of America

28 27 26   5 4 3 2 1

First edition

Contents

Translator's Note	*ix*
Foreword by Philippe Capelle-Dumont	*xi*
Preface by Jean Greisch	*xiii*
Editorial Note by Catherine Goldenstein	*xxiii*
Author's Preface	*xxv*
Introduction: Reflexive Method	*1*
PART I: LACHELIER	
Introduction	*15*
Naturalism and the Problem of God	*17*
The Formal God or the Idea of God	*35*
The Living God	*57*
PART II: LAGNEAU	
Introduction	*73*
I. Awakening Thought	*75*
II. The Conditions of Certainty: The Monism of Thought	*88*

III. Certainty and Action	*103*
Conclusion: The Method of Immanence and the Doctrine of Immanence	*119*
Notes	*131*
Index	*141*

Translator's Note

One challenge in translating this early work by Ricoeur was that the French term *esprit* plays such a prominent role in the work of the two philosophers he discusses, Jules Lachelier and Jules Lagneau. In their day, they would have been said to belong to the tradition of French philosophical spiritualism, a tradition that has to be understood in terms of its opponent: materialism, a mechanical and deterministic materialism, that was seen as eliminating freedom and denying the value of human existence. Talking about a philosophical spiritualism, however, does not convey to us today an immediate sense of what was at issue for them, particularly if English is our native language. We do use the word *spirit*: a spirited defense, the spirit of a place, the Holy Spirit—but spiritualism, were it to occur in contemporary English, seems to have more to do with spirits in the sense of ghosts than with what Lachelier and Lagneau meant by it. *Esprit*, moreover, is the word used today to translate "mind" in French translations of works on what English-speaking philosophers call the philosophy of mind. And from the point of view of that philosophy Lachelier and Lagneau do often seem to be talking about what these works call mind or the related "hard problem" of consciousness. So for the most part I have translated *esprit* as mind, but not always, for when Lachelier and Lagneau do talk about the metaphysical implications of their work and turn to what they want to call ultimate reality, absolute consciousness as a metaphysical reality—"pure spirit"—something more than what we call mind in English is at issue because spirit here goes beyond the mind–body or mind–matter distinction in that it includes both what we today call mind or consciousness and what they call nature or objective being.

A further complication stems from a conversation I once had with Professor Ricoeur. He was not someone who wanted to oversee or verify translations of his work. "It's your language," he once told me. But he loved language, as is evident from the important role discourse and the interpretation of discourse plays in his philosophy. And he loved puns both in French and English, and discovering new words as he moved between them. One winter in Chicago, it was the word *slush* that he just had to talk about as it was obvious there in Chicago what it meant, but as he saw, the idea and reality behind it were totally missing, and likely inexpressible, if not alien to French. More relevant to this volume, at another, much later date, he said to me, "David, you know what the French mean by *esprit* is not always what you mean in English by mind." Unfortunately, he did not go on to develop further what he had in mind by this, but it was clearly important to him—and meant as more than a caution to me.

In reading this translation, therefore, readers should keep in mind that when the word *mind* appears it always translates the French *esprit*, but sometimes the word *spirit* seemed called for, and there again the source word in French is *esprit*. The semantic fields of mind and *esprit* do overlap, but not completely. Perhaps one lesson to be learned from this text is that what we mean by *mind* in English is as problematic as is *esprit* in French.

Foreword

This work, which was originally written as a thesis in preparation for admission to advanced study by the young Paul Ricoeur in 1934, is the product of an old promise that the Ricoeur Archive has sought to fulfill and for which we wish to express our thanks. It is the result of a long editorial process undertaken by a collegial team, whose principal contributors were Jean Greisch, who provided the Preface; Catherine Goldenstein, who with Françoise-Emilie Jacqueline did the word processing and the required verification of the bibliographical quotations and citations; and, finally, Olivier Villemot, who did the final manuscript editing for publication.

It is a new expression of the participation by Paul Ricoeur in the series "Philosophy and Theology" published by Les Éditions du Cerf, to which he had already contributed the lecture he had given at the opening of the Nabert Archive in 2001, published as a postface to the volume *Jean Nabert et la question du divin*.[1]

The significance of publishing this text devoted to the problem of God in reflexive philosophy in a collection devoted to the philosophy of religion and particularly to the relation between philosophy and theology does not call for a long explanation. Publication of this text offers readers the chance to discover the extraordinary talent of a young philosopher and the thinking that was already taking form during a particularly dark period of twentieth-century history.

Philippe Capelle-Dumont
March 26, 2017

Preface

"The origin always remains in the future" (*Herkunft aber bleibt stets Zukunft*): this often-cited apothegm from Heidegger, in which he sums up that the ambiguous relation he held, along his path of thinking, with Christian theology does not apply to Ricoeur, who never was a theologian.

If we had to find an equivalent for Heidegger's saying in Ricoeur it would instead be what he said in 1952 about the "existential conditions of philosophical autonomy": "To begin from itself, philosophy must perhaps have presuppositions that it calls into question and critically re-absorbs into its starting point. Anyone who does not first have *sources* will not afterward achieve *autonomy*."[1]

Heidegger's saying is even less applicable to Ricoeur in that in his late work Ricoeur affirmed a philosophical agnosticism of a unique kind that prevented him from elaborating a fully formed philosophical theology, something however that did not prevent him from being interested in the potential intelligibility to be found in biblical exegesis.

We might wonder therefore whether publication of this thesis, which the young philosopher in 1934 devoted to the problem of God in two major representatives of French philosophy for whom the reflexive method provided the principle of an "integral metaphysics"—Jules Lachelier (1832–1918), to whom Bergson dedicated his *Time and Free Will: An Essay on the Immediate Data of Consciousness*, and his student Jules Lagneau (1851–1894), whose own most well-known disciple was Alain—is today doubly anachronistic.

xiii

Anachronistic, first of all, because those two twin stars of French philosophy of that day no longer burn so brightly in the heavens of contemporary thought, and in no way seem to help us to clarify the problems with which we currently are concerned. The same might be said of the constellation of names—Espinas, Boutroux, Cousin, Brunschvicg, Blondel, Bergson, Caro, Ravaisson, Baruzi, and so on—to be found in the pages of this thesis.

Anachronistic, next, because in his "intellectual autobiography" Ricoeur himself presented this text as the first truce in "the internecine war" between faith and reason that accompanied his philosophical itinerary from start to finish.[2] He concluded this reference to this work of his youth by adding that "these early incursions on the side of the God of the philosophers have remained practically without sequel,"[3] leaving a place for "a type of philosophy from which the actual mention of God is absent and in which the question of God, as a philosophical question, itself remains in a suspension that could be called agnostic."[4]

* * *

Nothing authorizes us, however, to conclude from this that his initial encounter with reflexive philosophy, to which would be added the more determining influence of Jean Nabert, was for Ricoeur a mere scholarly exercise, a quickly forgotten trial run.

Independently of the fact that in philosophy there are few encounters that do not lead to another day, Ricoeur himself states that the two Juleses not only "initiated" but literally "incorporated" him into the tradition of French reflexive philosophy.

To find the word *incorporated* (which must not be confused with *recruited*!) from the pen of a thinker who at just about the same time would be initiated by Gabriel Marcel into the mystery that incarnate existence is pregnant with significance and obliges us to ask about the way in which Ricoeur began by crossing the "line of a reflexive philosophy" by discovering in it a method that he never will deny, one that would have irritated his first teacher in philosophy, the Thomist Roland Dalbiez.

Talk about the "line of a reflexive philosophy" leads me to cite the formula from Ricoeur's article "On Interpretation" from the 1980s, which has been reprinted in a number of places and translated into many languages, in which he defines his belonging to the school of hermeneutic phenomenology by three features: "it stands in the line of a *reflexive* philosophy; it remains within the sphere of Husserlian *phenomenology*; it strives to be a *hermeneutical* variation of this phenomenology."[5]

Stands, remains, strives to be: the linkage of these three verbs is worth noting. Of the three orientations that determine the profile of what I like to call "hermeneutics *more gallico demonstrate*," the least contestable and most enduring is its belonging to reflexive philosophy.[6]

It will also have been noted that Ricoeur says that his philosophy is "in the line of *a* reflexive philosophy" and not in the line of reflexive philosophy. The indefinite article alerts us to the complexity of reflexive philosophy, which takes its starting point from the Cartesian *cogito*, then draws lessons from Maine de Biran, Kant, and Fichte before finding expression in the second half of the nineteenth century in the teaching and writings of Lachelier and Lagneau, whose book on *The Problem of the Existence of God* appeared in 1925, as well as in the work of Léon Brunschvicg (1870–1944), the tireless defender of the universality of Reason, which places judgment at the heart of reflexive philosophy, and, last but not least, Jean Nabert (1880–1960).

As Nabert would emphasize, starting from its Cartesian foundation, reflexive philosophy looks in two distinct directions: sometimes toward reflection on the conditions of possibility of true knowledge and, starting from there, to the universality of reason which prevails there; sometimes toward the inwardness of the life of consciousness that undergirds it.[7]

Kantian critique and Marburg neo-Kantianism favor the first option. Echoing Maine de Biran, the protagonists of the second option were more interested in the status of the subject, asking reflexive analysis to appropriate the concrete experiences that are solidary with the ego's destiny. "To promote a self-awareness which does not lack that dimension of intimacy which is absent from the transcendental consciousness of critical philosophy."[8] This concern, which lies under all Nabert's work, was equally Ricoeur's own.

From his side, Henri Gouhier distinguished two principal currents in the vast movement of French "spiritualism": the Bergsonian current, which favored the inwardness of life, and the Biranian current, followed by Ravaisson and Lachelier, who characterized his way of thinking as a "spiritualist realism" or a "spiritualist positivism," and Lagneau, not to forget Jean Nabert.

Much of Ricoeur's text suggests that in taking interest in the second rather than the first current, he made an initial philosophical choice, one that set him apart from Bergsonianism as well as from Blondel's philosophy of action.

* * *

In publishing Jules Lagneau's courses, his students pointed out that the reflexive method until then "was more celebrated than really known, except through a few hermetic formulas."

In presenting his own work as being above all an attempt at a historical reconstruction, Ricoeur makes an important contribution to the much-needed clarification of the real bases of the reflexive method. In doing so, he equally offers a first look at the idea he has about the work of understanding undertaken by the historian of philosophy. Even if he is the first audience for his work of reconstruction, his task was to make his reconstruction understandable to others, which comes down to outlining, through successive approximations, the philosophical attitude it incarnates.

By focusing on two personalities "who were opposed to each other in many ways to lay bare, through a kind of method of comparison and contrast, the root of their method and the fecundity belonging to each of them," Ricoeur invents an approach based on looking for differences that he will make use of often in his subsequent work, notably in his book on Gabriel Marcel and Karl Jaspers.[9]

In the present work, this way of looking at things brings to light the difference between Lachelier's approach which, according to a saying of Lagneau's reported by Alain, always had the Gospel at its back, and the primacy of the negative way through radical doubt which makes possible our certain knowledge of our ignorance. A similar doubt, Ricoeur adds, maybe speaking indirectly of himself, is not something pleasant but rather a form of suffering, that is, "an ascetic introduction to true certainty" much closer to the negative way of the mystics, of Saint John of the Cross's dark night of the soul, than to Montaigne's "what do I know?"

From the opening pages of this thesis readers will see that it presents a real piece of research. In it, the student makes use of Lachelier's unpublished papers and letters which Léon Brunschvicg had allowed him to consult. Noting the absence of a history of reflexive method, a lack that would magisterially be filled by Nabert in 1957, but choosing not to carry out research into the sources and influences that had an impact on his two thinkers, Ricoeur chooses to focus on their fundamental problem: "Research into the absolute about how, in appearance, it is most foreign" and what this means for religious philosophy.

What also holds his attention in the two Juleses' writings is the fact that both of them "found in reflexive method the principle of an integral metaphysics," which finds expression in a well-known formulation in Lachelier's article "Psychology and Metaphysics": "A being, such as we conceive it, is not first a blind necessity, then a will, which is bound up by this necessity in advance, finally a liberty which will have no other responsibility than to take note of these two. Rather it is wholly liberty inasmuch as it produced itself, and wholly will in so far at it produces itself as something concrete and real."[10]

The introduction to Ricoeur's thesis lays out the particularities regarding reflexive method that inseparably connect intellectualism and analysis. Ricoeur sees in this the expression of a radical intellectualism that is first presented as a methodological idealism that credits the intellect with the power of justifying itself. For this idealism, truth does not consist in the agreement of thought with an external reality, because it is the form of the true that defines the very structure of thought.

"Thought," declares Lachelier, "is the true, and the true is in the things themselves. That is where mind must look for itself if it wants to find itself, and if one says about it, following the Gospel saying, that it only finds itself in losing itself." Truth so understood is coherence, not correspondence, which implies, as Ricoeur underscores, that it is impersonal by nature and by definition.

Reflexive method as practiced by Lachelier and Lagneau was, Ricoeur notes in another brief document, probably prepared to accompany submission of this thesis, "an awakening, a call to clear consciousness, regarding the implicit and quasi-unconscious moves contained in the least act of thought." By moving back "from the conditioned to the conditions, from problems thinking had resolved to what they left unresolved," it comes, sooner or later, to the absolute.

Even if, and properly speaking when, it set off in quest of the absolute or God, the reflexive method refuses "to receive light from outside our thought." There is no salvation for thinking outside its clear and distinct ideas!

If the fact that reflexive philosophy belongs to the great phylum of intellectualism or idealism is beyond doubt, excluding by that very fact "every philosophy that reduces intellectual relations to sense impressions," it is a quite particular kind of intellectualism one is dealing with, if only because it excludes any recourse to an intellectual intuition.

The opposition between sensibility and reason is prolonged by another characteristic of this reflexive intellectualism that Ricoeur finds significant: the opposition between individuality and impersonality, an opposition particularly emphasized by Lagneau. A strict doctrine of immanence "leads the *cogito* to an impersonality of its rationality," at the risk of sacrificing "an essential feature of thinking, that it is a personal act." Being nothing other than an impersonal analysis of rationality, reflection cannot be confused with the *prise de conscience* of individual thought by a particular individual.

* * *

Is what gives strength to reflexive method—its decision to concern itself only with human beings in that they are minds, that is, a system of rational relations driven by nothing other than an endless progress toward truth—its Achilles' heel?

As can be confirmed starting with Descartes' *Metaphysical Mediations*, the apodictic assurance the *cogito* has of its own existence is the foundation of any knowledge worthy of the name, the *cogito* is not to be confused with the individual ego, such that reflection never really reaches the me.

Early on, Ricoeur was uneasy concerning the pitfall purely and simply identifying the person and the individual might contain. However discrete his protest concerning impersonal thought may have been, it is the basis for his commitment alongside Emmanuel Mounier to the personalism movement: "I am not just a mediocre novel of appearances and events; I am a drama and a destiny. It is my person that bears responsibility for thought, the burden of doubt, and the initiative of good will."

A drama and a destiny: these terms are laden with meaning and explain the importance of Gabriel Marcel for the young Ricoeur.

The least one can say is that he does not lack audacity when he starts by declaring that, despite the objectivity he claims for his presentation of his two authors, he also wants to track down their weak points, "the fissures the wedge of criticism might find an opening."

Even the greatest philosophers have their Achilles' heel. It is up to the interpreter to look for it, not to demonstrate that they are idols with feet of clay but to increase the chances for a real dialogue with them.

The reflexive method does not proceed deductively but through analysis, by "awakening," as Lagneau put it, "the latent thought in the smallest mental acts" which cannot be discovered by looking at an anatomical chart or by drawing the boundaries from an administrative point of view.

This refusal of artificial and abstract approaches equally determines the way reflexive philosophy approaches the question of God. Far from being a particular problem, thinking, as it has been defined, finds its real issue here.

By pointing out the criticism that Lachelier and even more Brunschvicg directed against Durkheim's reductive sociological approach, Ricoeur notes another important option concerning how to deal with the phenomenon of religion: it is not by first grasping religion as a total social fact, the expression of some group, but first of all as an inner effort of the soul seeking to give up everything other than itself, everything that is not an expression of its freedom, that one discerns the essence of religion. Reason alone, not society, is the guardian of true transcendence.

By noting the important debate about intellectualism and anti-intellectualism that opposed Brunschvicg and Maurice Blondel at the Congress of Philosophy in 1900, Ricoeur brings out a third particularity of the intellectualism underlying the reflexive method: precisely because the mind is active, it is not entirely transparent to itself, with the result that a conflict between richness and clarity is inevitable.[11]

This makes the wager that in 1950 opens the first volume of Ricoeur's *Freedom and Nature* all the more audacious: to honor equally "the two requirements of philosophical thought—clarity and depth, a sense for distinctions and a sense for covert bonds."[12] The same may be said about the dilemma of the intelligible and the immediate that opposes Lachelier and Lagneau to those who follow Bergson. It too lies in the background of Ricoeur's thought, which also is critical when it comes to any claim to immediate knowledge.

What matters for the reflexive method is being able to reflexively grasp the different acts through which mind really inserts itself in reality—by grasping it, so to speak, with both hands, however incongruous this expression may seem.

* * *

Can this peculiar type of analytic method, whose fecundity Lachelier began to test out in his book on induction, which consists in catching hold of thought in all its works, contribute to resolving the "problem of God," first of all by allowing us to reformulate it? This is the question Ricoeur addresses to Lachelier, then to Lagneau.

It quickly becomes apparent that the question needs to be reformulated, as will also be the case with Nabert's *Le Désir de Dieu*.[13] Reflexive philosophy cannot rest content with the question "What can I know about God?" if this comes down to adding a new proof of God's existence. For Lagneau, God, conceived of as the free affirmation of value, is sovereignly indemonstrable. Ricoeur draws a "broadly universal truth which overflows the framework of Lagneau's philosophy": the impossibility of introducing the absolute from the outside to a soul divested of it. Outside "the royal road of a free decision, whereby God reveals himself to be within us," all the roads to God lead nowhere.

Reflexive philosophy also protects itself against a God of the-gaps meant to fill the holes in human knowledge. Its quest for God takes place in the plain light of the intellect, focusing on the mind's many concrete successes, not through the poverty of pure concepts.

Far from reducing to a theoretical and speculative quest for being, reflexive thought is the practical ideal of a life reserved for those who consent to live through and by their intellect. Ricoeur concludes from this that, for these two authors who make the problem of God the directing idea of all their meditation, the use of the reflexive method is equivalent to a real conversion that rejoins the eternal problems of a good life, of beatitude, as in Fichte's *The Way Toward the Blessed Life*.[14] Precisely because this philosophy of spirit forbids itself from formulating human destiny in substantial terms, in terms of the soul, the problems of death and resurrection, are of little interest to it, being problems only for the imagination and the passions.

As Lachelier says forcefully, the philosophical God that the exercise of reflexive method must lead to, a wholly rational God, is nothing other than the infinite form of thought. It is only a second time, after having internalized the teaching of Kantian critical philosophy, that one can pass from the formal to the living God, the object of moral and religious faith.

Not wanting to give up either Darwin or Moses, Lachelier holds that religious faith cannot rest content and must therefore run the risk of committing itself to the living God, who is revealed to be a God of love.

For Lagneau, Ricoeur's second great interlocutor, this means that the highest act of thought consists in comprehending the necessity of positing the incomprehensible.

* * *

It is not the job of a Preface writer to tell readers how to read or to propose a ready-made interpretation of the text they are about to read. Leaving it up to them to accompany Ricoeur in his exploration of the new country of reflexive philosophy, I will offer just three brief comments.

(1) The page preserved in the Ricoeur Archive which recapitulates several "critical remarks" in light of the submission of this thesis once again emphasizes that, for Lachelier as for Lagneau, "the immanence of God to human thought rests on the impersonal character of thought." To Ricoeur's eyes, this impersonality risks compromising "the effort made to overcome a reification of thinking." In reality, he adds, "thinking is an act only on the condition of being personal. An impersonal act is contradictory. Worry, doubt, responsibility, certainty belong to a person."

This critical remark expresses a slight reticence as well. It reflects the idea that the young Ricoeur had of the human task which "is not perhaps to unwrap one's inner possessions, but rather to open oneself equally to other distinguished efforts than one's own, to accept collaboration with other beings in order to enhance one's own inner being."

Like Fichte and "his French successor Jean Nabert," Ricoeur holds "that reflection is less a justification of science and duty than it is a reappropriation of our effort to exist,"[15] meaning that "we must endlessly appropriate what we are through the mediation of the multiple expressions of our desire to be."[16] This requires the long detour by which "reflection is the appropriation of our effort to exist and our desire to be by means of *works which testify to this effort and this desire*."¹⁷

(2) The introduction to this thesis ends with a brief philosophical *credo* in which Ricoeur states what seems to him to be "the true perspective of philosophical inquiry":

> If the history of philosophy can sometimes be carried out as an autonomous discipline, and become a gratuitous erudition, it is normally the occasion for personal insight. If it is impossible to receive others' thought without its encountering latent directions in one's own consciousness which give rise to specifically personal reactions—in return, it is also not true that one can discover oneself without discovering others. One descends into oneself only by going outside oneself. One finds oneself only by losing oneself. One does not get to the Same except through the Other. Immanence always includes some transcendence.

Ricoeur not only never denied this *credo*, he continued to put it to work throughout his whole life.

(3) Also noteworthy is the fact this this thesis ends not with an affirmation, but with three open questions which Ricoeur addresses not just to himself but equally to the then-current generation of his readers:

> But are we capable of redoing what reflection has undone? Are we capable of surpassing that sterile freedom that opposes being and existence? Are we capable of that act "which at every moment realizes the world for us, which realizes it in the sense that, at every moment, the reality of the world is what we want it to be, that is, the result of a value we attribute to the thought in us, that is, to absolute thought"?

Knowing that Ricoeur's own philosophical itinerary ended with the outline of a "phenomenology of the capable human being," it can still be useful to meditate again on these three early questions.

Jean Greisch

Editorial Note

This *Mémoire d'études supérieurs* is conserved among the papers left by Paul Ricoeur and preserved at the Ricoeur Archive in Paris.

Directed by Léon Brunschvicg at the University of Rennes in 1933–1934, it was undoubtedly typed by someone in Ricoeur's family and submitted as 212 bound pages.

We have reproduced it as we found it, not adding notes to those that come from the young Ricoeur himself other than to fill in the details of the works he cited where he simply gave a title and page number.

The few explicative notes not from his pen are indicated by *editor's note*.

The pages cited sometimes contain errors. We have corrected them by checking them against the original texts cited.

All italics come from Ricoeur.

We have respected his punctuation. He uses semicolons, for example, more frequently than recommended by today's style, and he always liked using them. The many passages presented as new paragraphs are also characteristic of Ricoeur's style.

Finally, in many places the word *love* is styled with a capital *L*. We have respected this usage, even when it comes to quotations which in the original text use a lowercase letter.

Catherine Goldenstein

Author's Preface

A. This work is above all an effort at historical reconstruction. But, as with every subject in history, it is artificially removed from a larger background, and its borders are necessarily arbitrary. I have limited this study to Lachelier and Lagneau—not because they are the only illustrations of reflexive method, but because Lachelier and Lagneau are two thinkers who found in reflexive method the principle of an integral metaphysics. Others, such as Professor Brunschvicg, refuse to go beyond the horizons of a critique of judgment and a spiritual hygiene: "a geometer's consciousness of what is valid"—that is what philosophy is. Furthermore, these two personalities between them have sufficiently large differences that can be used to lay bare, by a kind of method of differences, the root of this method and its fecundity in their hands.

A complete study would require:

1. A history of reflexive method and a study of its applications starting from the oldest ones;

2. A second study close to the prior one, dealing with the actual sources and influences that decided these two thinkers' orientation. I have considered their philosophies uniquely in terms of what they achieved: that is, in their written manifestations. Thanks to the kindness of Professor Brunschvicg, I have had access to Lachelier's papers and been able to make use of unpublished letters that reveal the man's uncertainties behind the very assured literary production which is so complete when it comes to details. But the direct testimony of those who knew Lachelier and Lagneau and

attended their courses could help complete these inquiries into the background thought of these two great philosophers.

3. A comparison of these two systems with others that also makes use of reflexive method or others similar to it (that of immanence, for example).

I have not given the same importance to every aspect of these two philosophers: as my title indicates, I have looked only at the elements in their thought clearly directed toward religious research. Some studies of a more particularly logical or psychological character were judged to be less important. Nevertheless, the perspective of these two thinkers is in no way falsified by this stance; the problem of God was, for each of them, the directing idea of their meditation; their apparently quite different reflections serve to assure what is a fundamental undertaking, which is research into the absolute in what in it, in appearance, seems most foreign. From the very fact that to the eyes of Lachelier and Lagneau the Whole that is Thought is found in both these approaches, there are no autonomous problems or disjoint disciplines; there is just one problem, one discipline: a *prise de conscience* of the soul of all thought—that is, for them, God himself.

In my first chapter, I have tried to bring out the starting point of reflexive method, beneath the divergences in their application of it. Next, I have studied Lachelier and Lagneau separately, not without preparing along the way, a comparison with Lagneau. I have made more use of this comparative approach in studying Lagneau.

B. But, while I have tried to be as objective as possible in reconstructing these two systems, I have not confined myself to a strictly historical presentation. I have tried to discern the weak points, the fissures in which the wedge of critique might find an opening. Nor have I isolated these critical elements from the historical ones; but I have prepared, through some questions and hypothetical remarks along the way, the quite general lines of a critique I bring together in a few pages at the end of this work. This procedure has its inconvenient aspects; on the other hand, it does have the advantage of corresponding to the true perspective of philosophical inquiry. If the history of philosophy can sometimes be carried out as an autonomous discipline and become a gratuitous erudition, it is normally the occasion for personal insight. If it is impossible to receive others' thought without encountering latent directions in one's own consciousness that give rise to specifically personal reactions—in return, it is not true that one can discover oneself without discovering others. One descends into oneself only by going outside oneself. One finds oneself only by losing oneself. One does not get to the Same except through the Other. Immanence always includes some transcendence.

The Reflexive Method Applied to the Problem of God in Lachelier and Lagneau

Introduction: Reflexive Method

In publishing Jules Lagneau's course lectures on the existence of God, his disciples emphasized that the reflexive method was "until today better celebrated than known other than by a few hermetic formulas."[1]

For the students of a master teacher who had brilliantly illustrated this method, the best way of clarifying it was to make available for meditation the work that was "undoubtedly its clearest example": there was no other way to do so other than to reconstruct it from the start.

But for the historian who has to understand and reconstruct things for others, the best means of clarifying it perhaps is to outline, through successive approximations, the philosophical attitude it incarnates.

A

The most general attitude that characterizes these thinkers is assuredly idealism: whatever may be said about external reality, or rather about the mode of existence of what we call real, reality offers itself to us only under the form of elements of thought. We do not know what a thing in itself is which is not a known thing. This attitude may lead, strictly speaking, to realism, but, according to it, there is realism only as known as a conclusion. In the words of Professor Brunschvicg, "in the always open debate between idealism and realism . . . today it is idealism that holds the high ground, as the natural and immediate expressions of facts. What was paradoxical has become the necessary starting point of thought; there is no intellectual faculty that can be exercised apart from mind; the notion of external perception is a contradiction in terms. So the burden of proof lies with realism; to conclude in favor of realism means having to pass through the realm of ideas."[2]

We can speak of this starting point as a methodological idealism. The great drama about idealism is precisely a ceaselessly reborn effort to pass from this methodological idealism to a doctrinal idealism, to absorb the shock of what is external, the purely given, into the rhythm of thinking.

In an unpublished letter to Paul Janet (December 8, 1891), Lachelier characterizes this idealism in a broad way, ignoring the differences among thinkers: "It's Ravaisson, it seems to me, who has taught us to think of being not by using the objective forms of substance or phenomena, but by using the subjective form of mental action, where this action in the final analysis is thinking or willing. I believe you will rediscover this idea in Bergson and even in Ribot, as well as in Boutroux and my own work. And it is perhaps the one thing we have in common and that makes for the unity of the philosophical movement of the last twenty years."

This idealism Lachelier strongly affirms against the hybrid realism of eclectic thinkers, and against their intellectual intuition of entities inaccessible through our senses. He traces its origin back to Kant: "Whatever may be the mysterious foundation beneath phenomena, the order in which they follow one another is exclusively determined by the requirements of our thought. . . . Without any doubt there is nothing impossible in a principle, or in anything generally, existing without any communication with our minds. But at least it will be agreed that it is impossible for us to know anything about such a thing since nothing begins to exist for us except at the moment our mind enters into communication with it."[3]

It follows that an integral philosophy will be a philosophy of thinking: we have a first approximation of a method. Not of a sensation or an intellectual intuition, but of a redoubling of thinking on itself with a view to grasping its nature. This is how Lagneau means to demonstrate God. "The true moral proof is a proof that results from thinking reflecting on itself, in order to comprehend itself, to comprehend the necessities it obeys, when it tries to demonstrate the existence of God and the obstacles it cannot overcome in this demonstration."[4]

What still needs to be pointed out is the nature of this redoubling, this *prise de conscience*; we shall oppose it to a psychological method, whether one means by this introspection or philosophical intuition; we shall show that it presents itself as an *intellectual* consciousness.

Two series of precisions will singularly restrict the vast philosophical sector of idealism and circumscribe the starting point of reflexive method:

the first one will characterize the reflexive method as intellectualism, the second will characterize it as analysis—if we mean thereby the refusal of any *a priori* construction of mind, any deductive synthesis.

B

The essence of intellectualism is to define thought in terms of ideas, clear ideas. There are two versions of intellectualism. 1. If one denies the distinction or at least the autonomy of intelligence as regards the infra-intellectual; 2. If one posits the dependence of clear thought on something beyond the understanding irreducible to discursive thought and calls it life, invention, intuition, or even action, love. Between these two intellectualisms is the abyss that separates Hume from Bergson, Blondel, and Le Roy.

We are going to look at intellectualism in action on these two fronts.

* * *

The conflict with empiricism has implications much broader than one might first imagine: for intellectualism is opposed not only to every philosophy that reduces intellectual relations to sense impressions—but also to every philosophy that grants some continuity between concepts and sensations and makes what is intelligible an unpacking of sensation. This radical intellectualism therefore systematically opposes the understanding and sensibility. Undoubtedly, the intellect has need of sensation for appearances, but not when it comes to true being. Once constituted, the intellect finds its justification within itself and draws the criterion of truth from itself. The "true" does not reside in a reference to a thing but in an internal coherence. What is true is not the homogeneity of the thing and what is thought; it is a property immanent to thought, a form of thought: Lachelier and Lagneau constantly speak about the form of the true, as if it were a structure, a constitution that defines thought.

But if the true is what is rightly understood, if the true is immanent to whatever is intelligible, truth is fundamentally impersonal. The truth is not a feature of my individual thought: no doubt thinking only appears to individual minds, but the function of reflection is not to describe the individual modes of how things appear to thought, but their validity, their truth, their universal form. The presence of ideas stems from psychology, their validity comes from reflection. Reflection therefore is systematically opposed to introspection: from the point of view of psychological consciousness, everything is on the same level, sensations and ideas. From the point of view of reflection, there are, from the start, two parts to being human: what is universally justified, and what stems from individual sense experience. Thus, reflection immediately has to do with reason; it brings with itself a hierarchical concept of mind: "While the psychological method condemns us to skepticism, or if one prefers to subjectivism, the logical method, reflexive analysis liberates us from individual illusion by distinguishing what grounds us in reason."[5]

Consequently, reflexive method is not just any way of tackling mind; it brings with itself a stance, a point of view. A human being is of interest to it only as mind, that is, as a system of intellectual relations, progress toward the truth. To practice reflexive method is to posit the autonomy of reason with regard to sense experience.

This initial opposition between sense experience and reason brings with it a second opposition: that between individuality and impersonality. The reflexive method is opposed to investigations like those of Henri-Fredric Amiel or Proust. When I turn back on myself, in the way Lachelier or Lagneau do, it is not my own story I discover, but my universal nature: "We take into consideration only the mind's power of thinking, which is acknowledged by everyone to be identical everywhere."[6] Lagneau puts this even more strongly: reflection never encounters the ego: "This effort toward my mind is vain: the ego escapes, the universal mind is reached through the feeling of an absolute necessity both undergone and enacted, that is, as a total and absolute unity. The ground of things and their explanation does not lie in phenomena or in (necessary) objects, or in minds or (limited) subjects, but in the mind or the absolute and one subject."[7] "True psychology is not the description of some thought but the explication of Thought."[8] From this follows the capital assertion that Thinking is one, in the different minds in which it appears, and individuality a mirage: reflection, like its object, is impersonal. It is reason become conscious of itself: "Nothing is more personal in fact than philosophy, nothing more impersonal when it comes to validity, since it is total reality, that is, at bottom, if one really understands things, individual reason becoming aware of itself and rendering account of itself."[9] Reflection therefore is not the *prise de conscience* of individual thought by an individual, but an impersonal analysis of the intellect.

But the affirmation of the impersonality of thought also has another meaning: it is opposed not only to the thought of "my mind," but to the "I": the "I" as the center of an act, the "I" of the cogito. The partisans of the reflexive method often forget that I am not only an individual, but a person and they even systematically identify person and individual. However, I am not just a mediocre novel of appearances and events; I am a drama and a destiny. It is my person that bears responsibility for thought, the burden of doubt, and the initiative of good will. It will be necessary to ask what becomes of the person in the systems of Lachelier and Lagneau: it seems as though it has no place between the animal me and impersonal thought.

Let us note a final manifestation of reflexive intellectualism. Just as thought has nothing to do with sensation, nor with individuality, it is also distinct from the social and the collective.

Durkheim's sociology attempted to found the universality of truth on a concrete base, by reducing the universal to the collective. Lagneau did not know about the birth of sociologism; Lachelier ran into it at the end of his life. The echo of this conflict can be sought in the reverberations of this controversy at the Société Française de Philosophie: to Lachelier's eyes, society does not enjoy the transcendence that reason enjoys when it comes to nature; society is the world of passions. Moreover, rationality, which liberates us from the ego, may well appear in the solitude that removes us from the group: "Religion for the soul capable of it consists in an individual and solitary effort to free oneself and uncouple oneself from everything that is not the soul and from everything that, in it, is not its very freedom. . . . Religion ignores the group; it is an inner effort and, consequently, solitary."[10] Certainly it is in Brunschvicg's philosophy that this conflict between rationalism and sociologism reaches a peak.

* * *

We have opposed the intellectual to the infra-intellectual: to the sensory, the ego, the collective.

Now it is necessary to situate Lachelier's and Lagneau's intellectualism in regard to those philosophies that claim to transcend even the intellect. In fact, anti-intellectualism is a contemporary phenomenon. But Lachelier was well aware of it: his correspondence is filled with discussions about it with Espinas, Rauh, etc.

There is no better way to spell out the terms of the debate between intellectualism and anti-intellectualism than through what is found in the discussion that opposed Brunschvicg and Blondel at the 1900 Congress of Philosophy:[11] everyone agreed about one point, spirit is alive but not entirely transparent to itself. Around a luminous core extends, through imperceptible degradations, a vague shadow we call action and life; the goal is not difficult to state; it is necessary to spread as far as possible the clarity of reflection over the development of the mind. But how? Here is where the disagreement comes: do we install ourselves at the lighted center, in the region of clear and distinct ideas? Should we ignore the shadow as something given provisionally, destined to be absorbed into the clear ideas, and already consider the whole richness of thought to be clearly given? If so, we are intellectualists. Or should we, on the contrary, refuse this virtual assimilation of life and action and clear thought? Do we believe that the deeper experience of life reveals a plenitude that overflows understanding? If so, we will try to find a foothold in the fecund shadows through a method that, undoubtedly, will no longer be that of discursive thought but that will prefer richness to clarity. If so, we will have opted for anti-intellectualism.

We can go further: Bergson will present the understanding as a deformation; it will not be a question therefore of surpassing it, but of turning away from it. Its initial mistake is to take what is false as true:

> The importance of speculative reason, as Kant has demonstrated it, is perhaps at bottom only the impotence of an intellect enslaved to certain necessities of bodily life, and concerned with a matter which man has had to disorganize for the satisfaction of his wants. Our knowledge of things would thus no longer be relative to the fundamental structure of our mind, but only to its superficial acquired habits, to the contingent form which it derives from our bodily functions and form our lower needs. By unmaking that which these needs have made, we may restore to intuition its original purity and so recover contact with the real.[12]

Intellectualism invites us to break with the illusion of individuality and sense experience. Bergson invites us to go still further in this purification. Lachelier had already responded to this: formal freedom, which is the freedom of the very act of knowing, has nothing over against it [*pas d'au-delà*]. Its essence is to come last, or rather first.

Bergson will find a second vice in this intellectualism stemming from Kant: not only does it make the mind vassal to acquired superficial and useful habits, it takes the real target as the shadow and sacrifices the plenitude of the real to the poverty of the idea:

> Human intelligence, as we represent it, is not at all what Plato taught in the allegory of the cave. Its function is not to look at passing shadows nor yet to turn itself round and contemplate the glaring sun. It has something else to do. Harnessed, like yoked oxen, to a heavy task, we feel the play of our muscles and joints, the weight of the plow and the resistance of the soil. To act and to know that we are acting, coming into touch with reality and even living it, but only in the measure in which it concerns the work that is being accomplished and the furrow that is being plowed, such is the function of human intelligence. Yet a beneficent fluid bathes us, whence we draw the very force to labor and to live. From this ocean of life,

in which we are immersed, we are continually drawing something, and we feel that our being, or at least the intellect that guides it, has been formed therein by a kind of local concentration. Philosophy can only be an effort to dissolve again into the Whole.[13]

The intelligible or the immediate? This is the second dilemma for intellectualism and its adversaries. Lachelier and Lagneau made a clear choice: a return to the immediate comes down to positing the primacy of the given, the undergone; to transcend the intellect is to fall short of it: facts alone do not sustain themselves: "What exists for a man is not what is felt nor what we perceive. . . . It is that which one *must* perceive and feel in virtue of the laws of nature and of consciousness. . . . The intellectual consciousness, then, must draw from itself the light which cannot issue from sensible consciousness. We must possess, prior to all experience, an idea of what must be, an ideal being, as Plato would have it, which may function for us as the type and measure of real being."[14] Lachelier's intellectualism is quite firm about this: a philosophical God can be only a wholly rational God; when intellect no longer has anything to say, we are left with faith, which, eyes closed, affirms the risk of a higher anticipation. There is no middle term between a purely rational knowledge and a pure hope, a pure wager: "I have always been an intellectualist," he writes to Blondel, in 1896, "and my reading of Schopenhauer succeeded in setting me against the will and everything that has to do with it: like him, I became used to considering it a bad principle and to believe that the formal freedom and reason in us are the only points of contact with God's reality."

It is more difficult to evaluate Lagneau's intellectualism. Lagneau applied his efforts precisely to a critique of intellectual self-evidence: for him, the understanding is indeed a endpoint to get beyond, but love and action, which prolong it, are a higher incarnation of reason: love is what unites, whereas reason is the function of the universal. Everything that realizes the universal in us is therefore rational.

C

Having reached this point, a third order of precision imposes itself. What will be the starting point for a study of reason? Two ways present themselves: to start from the most fundamental idea and deduce from it the whole system of mind; the philosophy of spirit will then be a vast deductive system; its approach will be a composing of ideas, a synthesis—or we could start from the way mind [*l'esprit*] works, the concrete system of human thought, and return to the fundamental conditions of all the ways it gets realized: reflexive method will be an analysis—that is, a search for the condition starting from the conditioned.

What superiority did Lachelier and Lagneau see in analysis? Lachelier explicitly denies that a deductive system can impose itself from the start. To posit before ourselves an abstract principle prior to everything else is full of equivocations. What will guarantee it is true and not just the result of habit? What will assure us that it really applies to reality? This double problem of the truth of a starting point and its fecundity for knowledge will be resolved only if we begin precisely from where the problem has been resolved: it will be necessary therefore to start not from some possible knowledge but from actual knowledge, from a real insertion of the mind in reality, "how this item came to be found in our minds,"[15] "in one or in several concrete and particular acts by which thought constitutes itself while seizing immediately upon reality."[16] Reflection therefore is going to look for thought in its products; returning from the products to their production, it is going to look for the intellectual conditions of knowledge. It is necessary first of all to grant some success to thinking. There must be an initial given. For example, Lachelier starts from the inductive procedure that indicates the insertion of thought in reality: experimental knowledge is indeed one of those concrete acts through which thought constitutes itself in immediately grasping reality. Induction is taken as a successful fact: "No one has doubted the possibility of this operation."[17]

If we consider that using induction, mind starts from concrete knowledge and rises to a valid law for every time and place, the reflexive problem is as follows: "How is such an affirmation possible, and on what principle is it based?"[18] This is the meaning of the response Lachelier gives to Max Weber in their discussion about idealism and positivism: "Mind must not be sought outside the facts that it finds and through which it realizes itself. To construct the mind a priori would presuppose that thinking preexists things or could be something apart from them. . . . Thought is truth, and the truth is in the things themselves. That is where mind must look for itself if it wants to find itself, and one can say of it as the Gospel puts it, that it finds itself only in losing itself."[19]

From his side, Lagneau also condemned the deductive method: no doubt the deductive method demonstrates something. But it deals with the abstract, the possible: "Use of a deductive method leads to an abstract, formal psychology, a mathematics of pure ideas."[20]

There is more: the deductive method cannot account for its starting point. Does it posit it out of necessity? But the goal of the philosophy of mind is precisely to explain this necessity, to interpret and "evaluate" it.[21]

"There is no first fact." What is more, a starting point is all the more complex when it is taken as immediate.

So, the program of reflection will be to start from some fact and to explain it by Thought. Brunschvicg says something similar: "The idea of truth must posit itself in the fullness of its self-sufficiency, like a scholastic entity, and the scientist must be able to contemplate it prior to any intellectual undertaking, in order to orient his investigation."[22] The actual method will proceed not by deduction, but by reduction. This method, says Lagneau, "is both experimental, through its starting point, which is based on observation, and rational, by its very nature."[23] Or again: "Reflexive psychology presents the universal and determined character other forms of psychology lack."[24] The starting point, as Lachelier already saw, will therefore be a fact. So Lagneau defines reflexive method as: "Method (to explain thought) that consists in taking thought in terms of some one of its elements and seeking how we can comprehend this particular element in terms of the whole thought."[25] Rather than analyzing thought in general, we are going to take it by surprise in one of its works.

Brunschvicg will push this concern to look for thought in its concrete acts even further. He will hold that it is necessary to look at mind in its history. It is still too abstract in his eyes to posit induction, science, moral philosophy as timeless gains. Mind is not a nature given once and for all, but an evolving being.

But he does seem to have characterized the common starting point of reflection for the thinkers who have practiced this method: it is the "science of resolved problems." This is why it is an analysis, in the strict sense of the word: moving backward, a regressive study; each day problems get resolved: perception by the infant, science by the scientist, morality by the just person. Starting from their solutions, we can look for the why.

The reflexive method therefore does not dream of engendering reason but rather of becoming aware of it; Lagneau has an apt expression: we must "awaken" the latent thought in the smallest mental acts; "reflection does not create anything, it is a passage from the implicit to the explicit."

In short, the whole is in everything. Thought is a seamless being, which commits itself fully in each partial success. Lagneau had a strong sense of this unity of thought; one cannot separate problems any more than one can isolate oneself. The total presence of thought in every one of its works is as much the presence of every mind in any one mind as the presence of all thought in any one thought. It will be illusory therefore to chop up the difficulties, to divide in order to conquer; an anatomy of mind is a lack of insight. The publication of Lagneau's works itself confirms this conception of thought. The progressive development of a thesis always supposes a disjunction of problems. Thus it is not surprising that the whole book, for Lagneau, is in the first pages. No doubt there is some progress in *De l'existence de Dieu* for example, for development is the necessary price to pay for the human reality of time, and one cannot grasp a picture other than by clarifying its different parts in turn. But Lagneau's work appears more like the ebb and flow of changing points of view, which repel and rejoin one another.

Lachelier's work seems, at first sight, to contradict this conception of the unity of thought. He has a strong feeling of the discontinuity of points of view on being. There is no logical passage from mechanism to finality. This is correct. But these points of view are not equivalent, and mechanism is not, at bottom, a lack of insight. So long as the mind resides entirely on the plane of mechanism, this seems sufficient on its own terms, for there is, for it, no reason to surpass itself. But once, through an absolute step it raises itself to the level of finality, mechanism appears retrospectively as insufficient and incomplete. So we can say that reflection does not signify that thought is divided into autonomous realms, but also that there is nothing necessarily inevitable about deepening thought, passing from one plane of being to more consistent ones. Each new degree is implicitly present in the lower level, but the passage from implicit to explicit is spontaneous. While the aspect of unity is more evident in the compiling of Lagneau's works, the point of view of discontinuity is stronger in those of Lachelier. Lachelier has an extraordinary concern for details; he assures each progress in reflection with infinite care, as if to assure that the base should not be called into question; but at the end it appears that the summit was the foundation: "The movement of thought comes to a halt after being sought in necessity, as in its shadow, then in the will, as in its body, and being found finally in liberty."[26]

D

If this is what reflexive method is, it is easy to see that the problem of God is not an isolated question, one detached chapter of an ontology cleverly divided into autonomous problems. It is the problem of the Whole of thought.

Under the heading of idealism, God is the very being of thought; he is not to be looked for outside us, but in us; he is our better self, the soul of our soul; more internal to us than we are to ourselves.

Under the heading of intellectualism, this inquiry must start from the clearest corners of thinking. Inquiry regarding God begins in the full light of the intellect; the time has not yet arrived to consider that it must be prolonged by more than this. Here we are seeking only to assure a starting point.

Finally, under the heading of an analytic method, it is by drawing on the multitude of concrete achievements, not the poverty of pure concepts, that we must look for the divine act.

Let me add that this inquiry regarding God requires more than our knowledge. Idealism can be taken in two senses: thought is the theoretical principle of being; thought is life's practical ideal. Reflexive philosophy is the crossing point of these two points of view. Practicing the reflexive method is not a conceptual game, but a disciplined way of life. Speculating is not looking at a spectacle or regarding oneself in a mirror (*speculum*): it is consenting to live the life of the mind using the mind.

Spinoza, in his Dialectic of three souls, teaches that we are only what we affirm ourselves to be. The life of ideas cannot be pictured unless it is our very own life. "The ideas that define the conditions of truth and the good for the one who cultivates them and abandons himself to them are the soul of truth and justice."[27]

Lachelier says the same thing: "The act through which we affirm our own being wholly constitutes that being, for it is this very act which is realized and fixed in our character, and which is manifested and developed in our history. Hence it must not be said that we affirm ourselves to be such as we are; but on the contrary we are that which we affirm ourselves to be. . . . In a word, we achieve a destiny which we have chosen, or rather one we never cease choosing."[28]

And Lagneau will say the same thing: "In the final analysis, at each moment, we have the certainty we merit. The world in its reality is the exact expression of our own reality. For someone who, himself, has no value, it has no value. The meaning of things appears to us all the more clearly insofar as we augment our own value."[29]

Therefore reflection invites us to a choice, a real conversion. Will we turn to the life of the mind, or fall back into the illusion of individuality and the shadows of a life based on our passions? The choice is pressing, for it is the life or death of spirit that is at stake. Knowing ourselves to be spirit and yet to refuse the life of the mind is plainly contradictory: "Should we not make the effort to live life rather than simply undergoing it? Once again this is not a question that comes from our understanding: we are free and, in this sense, skepticism is true. But to answer no means making the world and ourselves unintelligible; it means decreeing chaos, first of all in ourselves. But chaos is not nothing. Being or not being, self and everything else, we have to choose."[30]

It is to this mental discipline that are joined the eternal problems of the true life, of beatitude. Reflexive method claims to be a method for reaching a happy life. It is a purification, an ascesis, a conversion. The originality of this philosophy of spirit is to perpetually refuse to pose the question of fate in substantial terms, in terms of a soul. The problems of death and resurrection are problems of the imagination and of passion.

Yet does our destiny come down to the realization of a mathematical deification? Do we end up with the strict rationality of the God of the integers? Must we believe that meaning owes its rationality to itself, that the supreme alternative is between understanding and not understanding; if so, "comprehending the alternative is having resolved the alternative" (Brunschvicg). Or does this ultimate choice suppose a mysterious power of action and life, perhaps even the initiative of a transcendence? Does this choice introduce us to something beyond the abstract notion of a mind, a beyond that goes beyond it yet grounds it? Lachelier believes that faith must risk giving itself to the living God who is revealed as love [*charité*]. If it is true that reason cannot lead us there, incompletion is our fate, the internal dissension of our nature warrants and legitimates this completing of the life of the mind on a plane which is no longer that of proof or of pure rationality. If it remains true that our philosophy is necessarily caught in our intellect, our inner life reaches beyond philosophy and opens itself to faith: there alone can the religious life be found. From his perspective, Lagneau is filled with this feeling that the Whole of our thought is not our understanding: "the highest act of thought definitely consists in comprehending the necessity of positing the incomprehensible."[31] The search for God prolongs itself therefore on a higher plane, that of right action and love, which as reasonable are no less of a higher order than is the world of ideas and mathematics. Since Lagneau does not believe at all in a revelation from this incomprehensible God, we must say that at the apex of our inquiry God remains incomprehensible, or rather that our inquiry has no apex. It is necessarily open-ended and incomplete. However immanent God may be, he always remains beyond what we can conceive through our understanding or realize through our love.

The problem is an important one. It comes down to that of the scope and limits of intellectualism. Does it really suffice that we install ourselves purely and simply in the universe of science and of justice? Does intellectual reflection have its end in itself? Or does it bring us face to face with an unceasingly renewed enigma, one that invites us to risk religious faith in a revealed God, or in transcending understanding through the most obscure anticipations—themselves condemned never to be saturated and exhaustive?

PART I

Lachelier

Introduction

Did reflexive analysis for Lachelier lead to God? How are we to know if we do not have some knowledge of this goal prior to application of this method? In fact, Lachelier was a Christian, and he lived practicing the faith of a Catholic. The problem arises in a quite special way: to what degree did he, through reason, draw closer to his lived faith? That is, a faith in a God distinct from the world, a God to whom one prays, who revealed himself to human beings? Without spelling out everything or designating one philosophy to the exclusion of all others, Christianity does point to some fairly precise philosophical directions, albeit supple ones.

Our approach will be to compare the successive degrees attained by philosophical reflection to the goal to reach.

I have used the word *degrees*, but it would be inexact to present Lachelier's thought as a linear development. It appears to have evolved from an orthodox Kantianism to an absolute idealism, and maybe even a third philosophy, that his care for perfection never allowed him to write. His letter to Paul Janet from December 8, 1891, bears witness to the first change of direction: with Kant, he continues to believe that things are not given in themselves, but rather grasped "through a kind of ideal setting constituted by a priori conditions, through the very idea of an idea and through the forms in which truth exists." But the metaphysical problem completely changes if this ideal setting is human thought, or if it is absolute thought. In the former case, we remain faithful to critical idealism, and the absolute still remains on the side of things in themselves; it transcends human thought, and we are always threatened with certain failure if, in turn, the path of practical reason is closed. It will be completely different if we turn to absolute idealism: the phantom of a thing in itself, transcending mind, vanishes; hence, "the only legitimate development of Kant's philosophy consists in saying that what is at issue here is not human thought, but absolute thought, and that the idea of being creates being, including what, in being, appears most real and most foreign to being." If so, "reason is a thing in itself," and God will certainly lie in this direction.

When did Lachelier move beyond Kant? Quite early, no doubt, perhaps even at the time of his thesis on "The Foundations of Induction." In a letter to Janet, he states that he did not dare go beyond Kant in his thesis, not knowing Kant's successors. Respect for his teacher must have lasted for a long while even given his doubts, and his not knowing anything about audacious post-Kantian developments held him back. But if the history of his evolution is unclear, the logical succession of dialectical moments is fairly easy to distinguish. There is a Kantian moment and an idealist one. The former corresponds to the thesis on the "Foundations of Induction," the second to the article "Psychology and Metaphysics."

Naturalism and the Problem of God

We know reflection's first move: we start from the mind's being inserted in reality: "Thought is the true, and the true is in the things themselves. This is where mind must look if it wants to find itself, and if one can say about it, following what the Gospel, that it only finds itself by losing itself." We have to grant an initial contact between thinking and its phenomena: a spontaneous knowledge, a real knowledge preceding reflection. We find the mind only as a condition of actual knowing and not as a nature in a pure state. To ask ourselves what the human mind comes down to seeking what role it plays in knowing what are the conditions of the relation between thinking and phenomena. In "The Foundations of Induction," Lachelier takes pretty much the approach Kant follows at the end of the Introduction to the *Critique of Judgement* (letter to Lionel Dauriac, November 16, 1887), which Émile Boutroux saw many times lying open to the same page on his desk. He defends an orthodox Kantianism: the order in our ideas is not a passive copy of things, whose conformity with the model, moreover, one cannot establish. To escape the radical skepticism of the empiricist's position, we are left with the Kantian hypothesis: the order of phenomena and that of our ideas are one and the same, in the sense that things, without being absorbed into the act that apprehends them, exclusively obey thought's requirements. Lachelier sees in the principle of induction the crucial experience that permits deciding the problem of knowledge in favor of Kantianism; the mind's role is evident there: in induction, the mind really does insert itself among things, for it is through its experiencing that it plunges into the plentitude of what is concrete: we cannot therefore charge it with being an empty framework, a word; but, furthermore, in induction, mind distinguishes itself from the concrete at the same time it immerses itself in it. Through a procedure whose possibility "no one has ever doubted," mind is allowed to go beyond its current experience to legislate for every time and every place.[1] There is more in the experienced idea than in a brute-given datum. It is in this hiatus between what is affirmed by the mind and what is simply presented to sense experience that the perspicuous insight of reflection is introduced. Here there is an actual gap between the idea and the fact, which warrants Kant's hypothesis: "Whatever may be the mysterious foundation beneath phenomena, the order in which they follow each other is exclusively determined by the requirements of our own thought."[2] In this privileged case, "the hypothesis which we are proposing is not merely admissible in itself, it is the only admissible one, for it alone allows us to understand how we are able to have *a priori* knowledge of the objective conditions of the existence of phenomena."[3] It alone answers the double question of necessity—the reef empiricism runs aground on—and the actual experience of mind of nature—the reef a theory of innate knowledge [*l'innéisme*] runs aground on—in short, the double question of truth and of the mind's fruitfulness: "[O]n one hand, we can determine these conditions absolutely *a priori*, since they follow from the very nature of our minds; and on the other hand, we cannot doubt that they apply to the objects of our experience, since beyond these conditions there is neither experience nor object for us."[4]

This is the critical idealism of the Foundations of Induction: "The conditions of existence of phenomena . . . are the very conditions thought."[5]

According to Lachelier, these conditions boil down to two laws: the law of efficient causes and that of final causes. The moment has come to ask ourselves what these two laws reveal about thinking. A study of pure mind will have taught us nothing. Induction, on the contrary, places us face to face with some concrete work of the mind, a problem resolved by thinking. In placing ourselves after the event, we are going to ask what the mind must have been in order to resolve this problem. This thesis does not seek to spell out the details of what Lachelier has to say about causality and finality, but to set them in relation to the problem of God.

Experiential knowledge of the world stems from two points of view: the point of view of causality, the point of view of finality. From the first point of view, knowing the universe means connecting phenomena in a causal sequence such that each term determines the existence of the following one. What must the mind be for the universe to be connected together in this way? To know is to unify, hence mind must itself be one.

But how are we supposed to understand this unity? Even for Victor Cousin, the mind behind phenomena, as a substrate knowable only through its modifications, presumes that these modifications are thinkable in themselves; as conditions, they put to work the subject that it is a question of reaching through them. And as regards Maine de Biran's hypothesis, it is no clearer, for the voluntary act is just a collection of muscle movements, without any particular unity.

Will the mind's unity then be that of a thought absorbed in its contemplation of itself? But this unity is thought about the universe as much as and even more than of itself. Furthermore, this unity is that of a form, a framework that is actualized only as a plurality; the internal interconnections among phenomena, the reciprocal affinity among sensations, that is the mind's unity: it is a unity incorporated in a diversity: "The question thus reduces itself to knowing what this connection consists in. It seems in this respect that we can represent it to ourselves only as an order of succession and concomitance, by reason of which the location of each phenomenon in time and space can be assigned in relation through its relation to the location of all the others."[6]

This necessary and *a priori* connectedness is the causal connection *par excellence*; it is what makes sense of necessity in science. What is more, insofar as it institutes the law of efficient causes, spirit explains the formal unity of the universe at the same time as that of phenomena as thought about.

* * *

Moving on from the mind's unity to that of things, we are going to seek for the general laws they must obey in order to be known; for our hypothesis is that the order in which phenomena succeed one another is determined exclusively by the requirements of our thought. If so, we should be able to deduce the concrete nature of these phenomena from the form of a law.

Unity in diversity, that was the mind's form when it came to the cortege of sensations, it must also be the material connectedness of the universe. "Further, a diversity in time and space is a diversity of state and position, both together. The unity of this double diversity can only be a continuous and uniform change of position, or, in a word, a continuous and uniform movement. All phenomena, then, are movements, or rather a single movement which goes as far as possible in the same direction and at the same speed. . . . Everything in nature is to be explained mechanically, for in a spatial-temporal world, a mechanism of nature is the only form of the determinism of thought."[7] This determinism allows for no exception or suspension: insofar as we ourselves are objects of inquiry, and not knowing subjects, we are phenomena like all other phenomena. Human beings are part of the universe of things, and their nature has no prerogative over other things: life and human freedom therefore do not escape from determinism. The hypothesis of a vital agent is unverifiable: "Perhaps the mechanism may be in some way informed by finality. We do not dispute this. In fact we shall prove it later. The only thing desirable to establish here is that nothing authorizes us to realize teleology in a special vital agent exempt from the general laws of matter and movement."[8]

Things are not different when it comes to human freedom: the freedom of indifference is contrary "not only to the supreme law of all experience, but also to the *data* of attentive observation."[9] It is not the wise man, but the capricious one who acts for no reason. What is more, an absolute freedom of indifference would make others' behavior an absolute enigma. But do we not predict their actions? The educator and the politician have a sagacity in this order that, for a few of them, almost reaches infallibility. Finally, statistics calculates the behavior of groups of men almost with a disconcerting precision. Lachelier sensed the later fruitfulness of what was to become sociological method and indicated the direction leading to a quantitative method for a science of social behavior. "There is even a statistics of crime by which penal legislation has to regulate itself in order to establish in each specific epoch a kind of balance between the violence of the passions which menace public security and the degree of fear required to control them."[10]

The point of view of efficient causes leads us to a vision of universal mechanism; we appear, it seems, to be encased in a kind of "idealistic materialism," that is, a conception of a purely mechanical world, dependent on an integrally intelligible mind.

But how are we to understand this *deduction* of mechanism and the idea of movement starting from the idea of causality? In what sense is the structure of the world dependent on that of the mind? It is a question here of a correspondence that Lachelier provisionally refuses to explain: his attitude is critical and not metaphysical. Below, we shall have to ask what metaphysics is appealed to here, whether some absolute upholds this correspondence. All that Lachelier affirms is that the law does *in fact* apply to phenomena; this application presupposes that "the law has to be the abstract expression of the phenomena, and in their turn, the phenomena have to be nothing more than the concrete expression of the law."[11]

Critique leads us to a raw given that metaphysics will in turn have to explain. Regarding this given: "through the mere fact of an object's existing for us, it must possess in itself a nature which renders possible the use of thought."[12] This is what critique says. Here is where metaphysics comes in: on what conditions is this correspondence realized? On what conditions do things depend on thinking?

* * *

Let us consider now a second aspect of the order of ideas and things that follows from this. The inductive process is not limited to subordinating a movement to an earlier movement, in another sense "it assumes, on the contrary, that the whole of these directions and speeds must be such as to reproduce that same combination at a given point. To say, however, that a complex phenomenon contains the reason for the simple phenomena which come together to produce it is to say that it is a final cause of the latter. Thus the law of final causes, quite as much as the law of efficient causes, is an indispensable element in the principle of induction."[13]

We shall not here undertake to develop this philosophy of finality for itself, or to criticize it, but rather to situate this new approach in terms of the religious perspective that is the guiding idea for this thesis.

For us, the great revolution that the finalist point of view introduces lies not in the defense of the principle of finality but in the fact that the human mind is not considered as a unique system but as a plurality of points of view and even, as we shall see, a hierarchy of levels. Let us say straight away, it is impossible to underestimate the implication of this point of view: this initial subordination of one level of thought to another permits us to envisage later ones. "By subordinating mechanism to finality, it prepares us to subordinate finality itself to a higher principle, and to cross, by an act of moral faith, beyond the boundaries of thought and nature."[14]

How does Lachelier demonstrate that the principle of finality is one of the essential bases of thinking? In truth, can we *demonstrate* the law of final causes, that is, prove that this law is a result, like that of efficient causes, of the relation of phenomena to our mind? Can this new unity of thought given the diversity of phenomena present itself in a perfectly intelligible form?

In fact, the exigence that pushes us to envisage thinking and the world from the angle of their harmony, their beauty and their art, is initially required to make sense of our sense experience: our first sense experience demands that living species and organic beings be taken into account. Or, to put it another way, it demands that there be an order to species, to things, a harmonious order. It bristles at the idea of an "infinitesimal dust, without figure, color, or property appreciable by any sense. Such a hypothesis seems exaggerated to us, and we are convinced that even when some particular law or other comes to be abrogated that a certain harmony would always subsist among the elements of the universe."[15]

But isn't there here just a confession of a strong emotional reaction? Can one speak of a law of thought? Undoubtedly, the law of final causes is foreign to the order of cold ideas, to the logical functioning of thought, to understanding. But thinking is more than understanding, it also has a concrete, aesthetic function, which is in no way a subjective mirage; but an objective and universal structure, in its own way. What this aesthetic function is, is something we shall have to consider when the time comes. If there is no rigorous demonstration of the principle of finality, we can, at least, demonstrate it through an argument from absurdity, show how impoverished logical thought would be, and, as a result, so too the world would be, without the richness of aesthetic thought.

If one considers the logical necessity that organizes the diversity of phenomena, one has to admit "that we have obtained by this means only an incomplete and superficial unity. For that which becomes one by means of this connection is not things themselves, but the series of positions which they occupy in time and the movement of thought which passes uninterruptedly from one to the other. . . . A thought entirely grounded upon the mechanical unity of nature, then, would slip in some way along the surface of the things without penetrating into the things themselves. Being external to reality, it itself would lack reality and would be only the empty form and abstract possibility of thought."[16]

Hence the law of final causes completes the law of efficient causes: this latter connects only empty thought and leaves everything concrete as irrational; the law of final causes unites a "real thinking" and a "meaningful reality"; it is the true synthesis of phenomena and thinking, of nature and mind.

Hence we must not visualize mind "as the causal connection of a spatial and temporal diversity, but as the totality of a living flow, they must be harmonious, or rather they should compose a melodic sequence in which the first chord vibrates to some extent in the last one."[17] It is difficult not to refer here to some pages from Bergson about *la durée*, and not discover in the opposition of mechanism and finality what Bergson institutes between spatial exteriority and the interiority of the *durée*, between geometrical thinking and dynamic thinking.

Now what must be the law of things that allows mind to apply the law of finality: "Every phenomenon, or what comes to the same thing, every movement is, then, the product of a spontaneity directed toward an end. But a spontaneity directed toward an end is a tendency, and a tendency which produces a movement is a force. Thus, every phenomenon is the development and the manifestation of a force."[18] The idea of force embraces every form of organization: that of the planets, of life, of consciousness, of human freedom: hence there is nothing original about the idea of life, or of consciousness: for "every sensation is the more or less indirect consciousness of the conflict of two forces." This new definition of nature takes nothing away from the previous one, it simply adds to it, for it does not have to do with the production of movement, but with its direction and velocity: force is a directed movement. We owe to Leibniz this insight into the continuity of the universe for which the idea of finality is really what connects things. Leibniz correctly recognized that: "Concentrated movement is precisely perception."[19] Force is a directive idea, as is life, but at a higher degree of perfection; consciousness is nothing other than a redoubling and human freedom a coming into bloom. The true philosophy of nature is a spiritual realism [*un réalisme spiritualiste*] to whose eyes everything is a force and every force a thought tending to a more and more complete awareness of itself. This is Leibniz's true heritage, why "it would be better to ignore Kant than Leibniz" (letter to Alfred Espinas, 1869). The moment has come to ask what Lachelier means by this aesthetic function of thought. He has given only a negative justification of it. A pure intellectualist, one who would make mathematics the ideal type of thought, might see only poetry in all this. And Lachelier's language lends itself to this: "Science so-called relates only to the material conditions of genuine existence and that this existence in itself is finality and harmony. Since every harmony represents some degree of beauty, however feeble it may be, beauty, let us not hesitate to say that a truth which is not beautiful is a mere logical game for the mind, and that the only stable truth which is worthy of this name is beauty."[20]

Poetic language, without a doubt: but the Beautiful is not the irrational, the Beautiful and harmony do not have, in Plato's eyes, the value of fiction or a lie. If poets must be excluded from the city, it is owing to the lies of their fables, and the immorality of their sentences.

Conversely, it is necessary to say that order is not just logical necessity; mathematics is not the highest law of thought, and Lachelier could have been thinking of Plato, who had nourished his thought, and whom he drew upon, when he wrote: "Thought which would renounce itself in order to lose itself, or rather in order to find itself entirely in the object, would come to know no other law than harmony and no other light than beauty."[21]

Let us go still further: this harmony, this beauty is not alien to the Good that illumines the world of ideas. The order of harmony is again what is most worthy and perfect, and it is not just Plato we can think of, but also Leibniz, who distinguished between logical necessity and the necessity "of the most appropriate choice." Thus we can say with Leibniz: "Everything which is, must be. However, strictly speaking, it could not-be. According to Leibniz, other possibles aspired to existence but did not receive it, not being perfect enough. Things exist both because they desire it and because they deserve it."[22]

Here we are at the heart of thinking, at the center of every explanation: "The good is the only thing which is the reason for itself."[23] Explanation through causes is necessarily incomplete, it is an infinite regression. "Thus, the mechanical explanation of a given phenomenon can never be completed, and an existence founded exclusively on necessity would present thought with an insoluble and contradictory problem."[24] On the contrary, explanation using final causes, the Good, permits positing that each end comes to a provisionally sufficient terminus. "If all explanation must move from a fixed and given point which is self-explanatory, evidently the genuine explanation of phenomena is not that which moves downward from causes to effects, but is on the contrary that which moves upward from means to ends."[25]

The meaning of this opposition must be the following: apart from the explanation which goes from one hypothesis to another hypothesis and never reaches an end, there is the explanation that moves from one postulate to another postulate. But there is a highest postulate. The law of final causes goes from one provisional postulate to another: indeed, each end-point has "an absolute value and could serve without absurdity as the limit of the movement of thought."[26]

If we grant that the law of final causes and the idea of the Good belong to the order of postulates, not hypotheses, we will understand why Lachelier makes the law of final causes depend on an act of the will: A "purely abstract existence would be, so far as thought is concerned, a state of illusion and death. It has, therefore, to draw on its relationship with reality, life and the feeling of its own being, which decides to do by an act of will, not of knowledge."[27] Thinking does not exclude willing: this is precisely the meaning of the notion of a postulate.

The incomplete character of explanation in terms of ends by itself suffices to give preeminence to mechanistic explanation. Lachelier does not hesitate to see in it an insufficient substitute, "a necessary hypothesis or rather an indispensable symbol[28] through which we project into time and space that which is superior to both."[29]

But then, if the understanding is subordinate to the will, is the moral demand so to speak that life posits more profound than the geometrical necessity that grounds mechanism? This is an unexpected perspective for an intellectualist philosophy: the will founds the true knowledge of the world.

But let us look in another place for clarification. In the *Vocabulaire Philosophique*, having defined thinking, he protests against the Cartesian assimilation of the rational and the mathematical or mechanistic: "On the contrary, nothing is more in conformable to *reason* than the existence of a reality, full and impenetrable by the *understanding*, a nature, a life, a sensible awareness, by feeling its way, so to say, and moving from one unforeseeable form to another . . ."[30] Therefore it is reason that, beyond geometric understanding, institutes finality: the problem becomes more complicated rather than clarified. What is this reason? What relation does it have to the will?

One can surely ask whether Lachelier did not find himself cramped by intellectualism and whether he did not respect its language in breaking its framework: this demand life poses resembles that deep drive of thinking that Edouard Le Roy calls thinking-action and is willing if we hold on to the aspect of momentum, or reason if we focus on its direction. Analysis of this deep-seated willing uncovers an aspiration toward the better and the affirmation of a highest value. The world is oriented toward perfection.

Despite the repugnance Lachelier always showed for Le Roy's language, he seems to say the same thing when he repeats with Leibniz and Bossuet that it is necessary, in a more than logical sense of the word, that the better should exist (letter to Jean Jaurès, February 6, 1892). Just as Le Roy suspends the world of clear ideas and mechanism from the world of invention and creation oriented toward perfection, Lachelier will say, from his side, that logical necessity: "presupposes that intrinsic value in virtue of which the ground of being claims to be and prevails over nothingness" (letter to Frédéric Rauh, February 13, 1893). What is more, Lachelier himself talks about a "spiritual-action" to designate life's demand we impose on the universe:

> Spiritual action, tendency (which is for me the same thing as finality), cannot arrive at the same degree of clarity as does determinism, which is the understanding dealing with things. . . . The real as such and as it is opposed to logic, is for the understanding a real stumbling block, a scandal.
>
> But what is not justified to the eye of the understanding, does justify itself, perhaps, to the eye of reason. And if there is something rational, it is undoubtedly that there should be something real, living, good, happy, and not that everything is logic and pure indifference: being is better than nothing, Bossuet said (letter to Janet, December 2, 1891).

Here is the type of affirmation not attributable to the understanding.

Therefore it is to a real trial of the understanding, in the exclusively logical sense, that these pages seem to lead. The understanding is, no doubt, not a slope to reclimb, a deformation that must be corrected, as for Bergson, but a point of view to surpass. Let us add that Lagneau will pass through the same criticism of mechanistic explanation. He will say that there is no first fact. But, at the moment when Lachelier introduces a higher type of explanation, and when he indicates the direction of an effort meant to introduce us to pure beauty, Lagneau declares that it is the very idea of a total explanation that is contradictory, and the case against explanation leads, not to an aesthetic philosophy, but to radical doubt. This by itself is sufficient to establish an important opposition between these two ways of getting beyond mechanism.

* * *

Where are we on our path leading to God? One point has been acquired: we have assured the objectivity of the world, but, in return, it seems that we have turned our back on the goal we are pursuing. To save the world, we have lost thinking; we have made the universe the immediate organ of the mind [*l'esprit*] and, in so doing, fused thinking to nature. We have buried mind: it is the form of an indispensable matter.

The *raison d'être* of Lachelier's thesis was clearly to place the accent on the first character: the objective value of the world; the goal of this work, on the contrary, is to place the accent on the second character: the degree of the mind's independence from nature. Therefore it is the photographic negative of the same system that needs to be looked at.

Lachelier's principal objective was to justify the necessity of science, or, what is the same thing, the objectivity of the world. It was a question of overcoming the skepticism that is the normal outcome of empiricism and of Victor Cousin's eclecticism. At bottom, this is a goal identical to what Kant proposed, and it is through inverting his preoccupations and intention, as we are proposing to do, that Kant has been judged to be a skeptic: he is a skeptic only in relation to a metaphysical and religious ideal: in relation to what he sacrifices. But, like Kant, Lachelier can flatter himself for having assured to phenomena "the only explanation we are able to give for their objective existence."[31] Their objectivity is of two kinds depending on the double point of view under which we can place them: that of geometric necessity, and that suiting aesthetics and moral philosophy. So, it is necessary to renounce an objectivity of the world founded on the alleged evidence of our sensations. It is even to renounce the privilege of the sensations of making an effort (Maine de Biran), which are no less subjective than any other sense data: in the order of sense experience, existence remains "quite subjective and relative to our individual sensibility."[32] The objectivity of the world rests even less on substances that we do not sense; for the thing in itself set apart from becoming vanishes as unknowable: "phenomena which for us at least are merely sensations."[33] The world's objectivity does not lie in an exteriority of a corporeal or spatial type; it lies wholly in one or another form of necessity for our knowledge. Kant has defeated Hume: objective idealism is the only system capable of triumphing over skepticism. What is more, realism carries the seed of skepticism, for the object cut off from thought about it always escapes knowledge: thinking cannot go outside itself to apprehend something alien to it: "Dogmatism is skepticism."[34]

So the objectivity of the world does not start with science; the heavens contemplated by a layman are relative to his point of view, but the astronomer, by situating the solar system in an objective system, detaches himself from the subjectivity of a point of view. "This is knowledge like God possesses."[35]

Consequently, there can be only one mind [*esprit*] but several meanings, just as there is only one world, but a plurality of points of view on it. The impersonality of thought and the objectivity of the world are one and the same.

From the point of view of mechanism, the world's objectivity is nothing other than science's necessity. "Movement is the only genuine phenomenon just because it is the only intelligible phenomenon. Descartes was correct in saying that every clear idea is a true idea, for the intelligibility of phenomena is precisely the same thing as their objective existence."[36]

From the point of finality, "a phenomenon *exists* inasmuch as it cooperates in realizing an ideal end."[37]

In both cases, existence is identical with the apriority of a law. Finality is no more concrete than mechanism; it is known in the same way: a rule for constructing the world.

We can then conclude that order alone in its two forms is objective, and that its objectivity lies wholly in its geometric necessity or in the suitability that the mind encounters in thinking it. The first thing reflection does is give us a world in giving us knowledge.

But let us consider the counterpart to this, which is what is of interest to us: if the objectivity of the world lies in its identity with the laws of the mind, conversely, "from its own point of view, however, thought is nothing but the necessity which constitutes the existence of phenomena. . . . But in the world of phenomena whose center we occupy, thought and existence are two names for universal and eternal necessity."[38] It is as true to say we are immanent to the world as to say it is immanent to us. The world does not depend on us, of course, but neither is it outside us. Objectivism is not a realism: as a result, there is not, properly speaking, a numerical distinction between mind and things. "Thought about phenomena is the same thing as their objective existence."[39]

Irreducible to sensations and individual experience, the world is immanent to spirit; its whole consistency rests on the apriority of the law that mind applies to it. But, on the other hand, spirit is just the causal or final interconnectedness of the universe. Critique, which dissociates objectivity and exteriority and which has put an end to skepticism, binds the mind to the world. Our personal identity is just the unity that holds together the world: "It is this logical unity that is the true support for consciousness of our personal identity. Otherwise, we have the incoherence of what is external and the madness of what is internal."[40] The framework of thoughts is the framework of objects.

Lachelier clearly felt that his thesis could change his deepest intentions. Thus he thought of writing a thesis in Latin on the foundations of moral philosophy to serve "as a correction to the exclusively naturalist conclusions of my French thesis" (letter to Émile Boutroux, August 8, 1869).

But, someone may say, this naturalism is rigorous and radical only from the point of view of mechanism: does not finality introduce, as Lachelier himself admits, a kind of spiritualism? Here, once again, it is necessary to look at the negative side of what has been accomplished so far: finality is a universal law and does not isolate us from the world. Nature as a whole tends toward consciousness and freedom. It is therefore more exact to feel regret that our freedom is *merely* the highest form of the work of nature. It is more exact to compare human invention with the universal invention of life than to oppose their rhythm. "Nature gives evidence of a sort of liberty every time it produces a new kind of organism by its own efforts and without a model."[41] For animal species, this invention has to do with their organs; for man, it lies in the power to vary one's plans and to conceive new ideas. Whereas the bird builds its nest, "which is a kind of extension of its own body . . . the privilege of our intelligence is to invent in its turn and to conceive an infinite number of pure ideas which our will then undertakes to realize externally."[42] Freedom therefore does not detach us from nature; with it, we achieve a work drafted by the whole universe: "The miracle of nature within us as without us is the invention and production of ideas."[43]

Writing one day to Espinas (May 30, 1869), Lachelier took pleasure in finding in man a kind of magnification of how nature works: "The work of literary composition, by which we first conceive everything (the truth to be demonstrated, the impression to be produced), then the parts (reasons, images), then the details of these parts, gives us a pretty exact idea of these natural creations."

Will someone not object that what is proper about man is finally to reflect on these tendencies, to clarify them through thinking about them? But this thinking was itself gestated by nature: "The movement concentrated in force is precisely perception as Leibniz defined it; that is to say, it is the expression of multitude in unity. It could be maintained, then, that there is no force which does not perceive itself perceiving the movement it engenders."[44]

The human soul is just the final stage of this concentration of material forces that gave rise to life; the soul is just "the dynamic unity of the perceptual apparatus, just as life properly so-called is only the dynamic unity of the whole organism."[45] This leads to the conclusion: "This soul which is identical with the things which it represents and which, according to Aristotle, is only the form of forms, is not that which we expect to preserve eternally; however, this sublime hope can be justified only by moral considerations which are quite foreign to the subject of this study."[46]

If the soul does not lie in this direction, how can God be there?

* * *

Does this mean having to say that this first approach to reflection is completely negative? Having set out in search of God, have we found ourselves completely at a dead end? No; the very progress of the dialectic, from mechanism to finalism, invites us to continue along this way: "This second philosophy is independent of religion, but by subordinating mechanism to finality, it prepares us to subordinate finality itself to a higher principle and to cross, by an act of moral faith, beyond the boundaries of thought and nature."[47]

Locked within the unique plane of mechanism, thinking was unable to envisage another explanation of the universe or of itself; finalism brought about a kind of liberation by inviting spirit to pursue this work even beyond finalism.

But one decisive reason is going to prevent us, provisionally, from finding God in thinking about the conditions of thinking.

In faithfulness to Kant's critical idealism, the conditions of thought are only human rules: thinking is not a thing-in-itself and God cannot be the absolute reality of the thinking subject. The thing-in-itself transcends our mind, and God is on the side of the thing-in-itself. So long as we remain within a strictly Kantian perspective, God cannot be sought within the way of radical immanence, but only through that of radical transcendence. The sterility of reflection is the exact consequence of the survival of the thing-in-itself. Renouncing attempts to find God in what is best about ourselves lets us, with Kant, provisionally set absolute freedom, the soul, and God apart from the vicissitudes of phenomena in the unattackable world of the "noumena."

Lachelier's letters bear witness to the fact that he paused for a while with the idea of a radical distinction between "noumena" and "phenomena." There is certainly something reassuring about maintaining the existence of a noumenal world even while declaring it to be unknowable; provisionally, it is an elegant solution, one filled with a sense of security: "I believe that between science and faith," he writes to Elme Caro in 1882, "the contradiction is unsolvable if they are both placed on the ground of phenomena. And I am inclined to extend to all the solutions of this order the solution that Kant gave to the problem of freedom. . . . The moral law will be no less absolute, when even as historical it comes about one day through a gradual refining of our instincts. . . . I am with those who do not want to abandon either Darwin or Moses."

Another time, he will say to Boutroux (July 14, 1877): "With Kant, I have always believed that freedom has no place within the domain of experience, and that it cannot be the cause of anything, although it ought to be and must be, in another way, the cause of everything."

But do we have any reason to affirm the existence of this freedom and this God? Because this noumenal world so resembles what Victor Cousin called the substantial world, which one has set aside, it seems as though it does not exist at all for us.

But for this not to be the case, we must turn away from the indications of nature: "I am far from believing," Lachelier writes to Espinas, whose organicism he criticizes, "that freedom is just a higher form of art, of nature, or of human society, a hive or a factory. I have expressly stated in my thesis that I will only talk about freedom from an aesthetic point of view and that I will set aside all moral considerations; and I believe these considerations are so important that everything else counts as nothing in comparison to them" (February 1, 1872).

Should we then follow Kant along the path of practical reason? Will God be a postulate from which duty follows? First of all, does this notion constitute a sufficient starting point? No: Lachelier does not believe that the law of justice is sufficient unto itself; on the contrary it rests on love: "The fundamental notion of society is not that of justice, but of love. Laws are a necessary evil. . . . Justice itself would not last very long in this world without love" (May 4, 1871).

Here is the starting point for shaking off Kant. Does he not write to Caro: "The categorical imperative, however respectable it may be, is perhaps not the last word when it comes to moral philosophy. I would not be reluctant to subordinate the law to grace, justice to love"? (February 1, 1872). Therefore it is possible to go beyond the idea of duty.

If duty is: love more than justice, might we, at least, get to God as the condition of its realization and sanction? This way never seems to have tempted Lachelier: duty is not an indispensable starting point for him and is not sufficient by itself. Duty is instead a point one arrives at: it is not a springboard that allows us to rise up to God, but rather an attribute of faith in God, the actual realization of that faith.

The course on logic from 1866 to 1867 presents moral philosophy as a deductive science—not in the sense that duty ought to be subordinated to something other than itself, but in the sense that good action requires a principle that confers an absolute value on it. In a still more energetic way, in the article "Philosophy" in the *Dictionnaire philosophique*, he considers morality to be the principal corollary of philosophy.[48]

Good action will be action that symbolizes the unity and spirituality of God. Duty will consist in "realizing in ourselves the relations that most faithfully represent what exists in the supreme ground."[49] Taking for himself the words of the apostle: "Become imitators of God" (Ephesians 5:1), Lachelier subordinates duty to the knowledge of God more than as arising from our duty to God.

It remains the case that belief in God is itself a moral act and not a distinct postulate, and that we settle two problems at the same time by one supreme decision, by an ultimate act of faith. Does this act of moral faith announce the end of the argument that, going beyond the clarities of reason, "crosses the boundaries of thought at the same time as those of nature"?

The moral act, in positing without proof that the ideal world is what it is, practically affirms the existence of a being outside our moral conscience.[50] God and the supreme value of the God will be the object of one and the same act of faith, of one and the same risk to be taken. This will be the meaning of that "purely spontaneous and philosophical act of freedom and faith," he speaks of to Felix Ravaisson (May 4, 1871). But we must not fear falling into subjectivism and fideism and negating the condemnation brought against the will in the name of a strict intellectualism, for "among the truths we will, if one can speak this way, there are those we will without being driven by any inclination, like the existence of a future heavenly city, they relate to a supersensible order" (letter to Espinas, July 17, 1871). These truths are the object not of a desire but of a free will.

But is this solution satisfactory for someone fixated on unity? Can we content ourselves with juxtaposing a thinking fixed on nature and a faith that is liberating but that remains opaque to thought? Lachelier did not believe so. In the same letter to Ravaisson, he proposes a second hypothesis: "Morality, like religion, which I do not separate, seems to me essentially the science of immortality. Now, how can we, somehow, penetrate to the immortal portion of ourselves? Is it through a purely spontaneous and philosophical free act of faith? Or does consciousness of our freedom give us only the idea of an absolute in general which we will be unable to determine and chimeric, if a revelation properly speaking did not come to teach us the substance of this absolute is charity? This is, I believe, the point on which all the others depend and around which my thoughts have circled for a long time without being able to pin it down" (letter to Ravaisson, May 4, 1871).

Will reason therefore have the power to sketch the very general and indeterminate framework of the rational elements of this science of immorality that faith must then nourish to be fully alive? All of our thinker's thought will henceforth be pointed in this direction: beyond naturalism and science, to lay the metaphysical groundwork upon which moral faith can blossom: already in 1868 he had written to Ravaisson: "I have always believed and still believe that we have an awareness of infinity; what I noticed, in reading Kant, was that we are conscious of a formal or intellectual infinity, but that the material infinity or existence is necessarily foreign to our consciousness just as it is distinct from the universe. How, then, I asked myself, can it be for us an object of faith? I answer that it suffices that we conceive it as possible, for once such an idea appears to us, we are absolutely obliged to will it to be a reality and to act upon this assumption. For me, it is through this decision of the will that a moral faith consists, which is not a *fides ex auditu*, but which can, in turn, serve as its basis" (August 16, 1868).

This important declaration, contemporary with and even prior to Lachelier's hesitations, will however remain the leading thread of his thinking. In the first place, it will be a question of attaining that formal or intellectual infinity, which is the philosophical God, and then, to pass from this formal God to the living God, the object of moral and religious faith.

But the philosophical problem of infinity will remain practically unsolvable so long as we have not got beyond the Kantian perspective. To this point, reflection has bound us to the human mind. Infinity did not lie on this side but on that of the thing in itself which transcends us. The problem will be resolved the day we dare to see infinity in our absolute power of thinking: then, reason will be a thing in itself, infinity will be in us, will be us, the best of us, and it will be through deepening reflection that we shall reach God in us.

At the same time, the relation of mind and things will be posed in a wholly new way: we must no longer speak about a correspondence of things with the human mind; the preestablished harmony that critical thought postulates but does not explain must turn into a relation of dependence, if not of identity. This thesis is necessarily connected to idealism. If the power of thinking which is in us is absolute, the real is a function of this.

But before handing over this new impulse to reflection, it is necessary to demonstrate that the Kantian critique of the idea of God was not totally without value.

Kant demonstrated the inability of reason to reach the ground of things; it exhausts itself in unavoidable antinomies and must renounce legislating beyond actual experience. Lachelier readily grants the inanity of traditional demonstrations of the existence of God, but he seeks to take up the torch and bring to light the useful value of the Kantian critique.

Without a doubt, we must renounce grasping God as the cause of the world or the basic substance, for these two principles have no value within the framework of actual experience; but if we pay attention to what we gain and not to what we lose, we will see that Kant has purified the notion of God: the principle of causality risks making him a primitive state of the world; thanks to Kant, we have detached God from the *intramondum* ideal of perfection. In a letter to Jean Baruzi from 1906, Lachelier strongly emphasizes the fecundity of Kantian critique: contrary to Leibniz, Kant reduces everything that is to the rank of being phenomena; what is beyond them is undoubtedly unknowable for us in our ordinary life, but through this, Kant has purified the very idea of the unknowable. He has shown us that God is not what the realists believe him to be, a kind of *totum* or even *summun* of reality, a "kind of reservoir of reality" (letter to Jean Jaurès, 1892), in brief, a hyper-space. Thanks to Kant, God can no longer be the substratum of what is real. From now on, he is *above* reality; he is "idea, pure law, what ought to be. . . . I am not saying that God is being, and I am not saying either that he is only an idea, I would rather say that he is beyond both of these and of everything we can conceive of" (ibid.).

Kantianism therefore rejoins, in Lachelier's eye, the *via negativa* of Dionysius the Aeropagite. It is a true ascesis, similar to that "dark night of understanding" of which Saint John of the Cross speaks.

But the Kantian critique of the idea of God cannot turn out to be something useful unless we are capable of redoubling this negative language into a positive anticipation. We will not be able to pick its fruit unless God is transformed for our eyes into a purer vision of what he is. Does Kantianism allow this? Do we have an idea of the infinite? Yes, for if it is true that reason does not resolve the problem of God, it is at least beyond the understanding, the faculty that poses this problem. Already on August 8, 1869, he writes to Émile Boutroux: "No doubt, Kant is correct against our eclectic thinkers and even perhaps against Descartes when he maintains that we have no intuition, no real and positive knowledge of infinity; but he does at least admit the problem of the absolute, beyond the understanding, a faculty whose function is precisely to provide us with its idea, that is, to pose the problem, whatever the inability of the understanding to resolve it may be. It seems to me that, above all else, it is necessary to acknowledge the existence of this idea, which marks the place for a future intuition, even while allowing that the notions that people believe themselves to have today of God are merely chimeras" (letter to Boutroux, August 8, 1869).

The Formal God or the Idea of God

The mind's reflection on itself has led so far to an impasse. The ideal milieu of categories through which things are reflected imposes a human cloak on them in giving them the stamp of objectivity. We have been left impotent to find anything other than ourselves and our human truth in the organization and order we introduced into the universe. We shall have no chance of finding God in this direction unless we get beyond Kant and if we dare to say that the thing-in-itself is reason itself. As a result, far from thickening the veil that conceals reality from us, reason will be the absolute root of reality. What is necessary for us will be necessary in itself. Truth will no longer be "something subjective and in a way provisory" (letter to Rauh, March 10, 1893). Kant's mistake was "leaving subsisting, beyond reason, the possibility of a thing in itself" (ibid.). Kantianism, undoubtedly, was an objectivism, in the sense that it removed truth from the arbitrariness of individual imaginations. It remains a subjectivism in that it made knowledge subservient to purely human rules, and in sum falsifying, leaving the ideal of a truth that would be the agreement of thoughts and things, along with the thing-in-itself, out of reach. The day this realist mirage disappears, human knowledge loses its provisory and subjective character and becomes absolute knowledge. With absolute idealism, the antinomy of a purely human knowledge and an unknowable absolute dissolves into the identity of the absolute with knowledge.

Hence, a direction is imposed, excluding all others: to get to the root of human thinking in order to find the absolute: "The legitimate development and the only legitimate development of Kant's philosophy consists in saying that it is not a question of human thought but of absolute thought, and that the idea of being creates being as a whole, including what, in being, appears to this thought as most real and most foreign to being" (letter to Janet, December 8, 1891).

* * *

The program of reflection is twofold: 1. to look for the absolute ground of thinking, that is, God; 2. To show that all being proceeds from its being abstractly posited by thought; in other words, to make the idea of God and that of the world stem from a reflection on the absolute conditions for any thought. The second problem is just as interesting as this first one, for the deduction of real being is an indispensable verification which no absolute idealism can avoid; if reason is a thing-in-itself, it will not be truly absolute unless everything is internal to it—that is, if it is not just the form of but also creative of its matter, if sensibility is absorbed in one way or another into the rhythm of absolute thought: an awe-inspiring demonstration which critical idealism is not required to provide, for it claims only to trace actual knowledge back to its formal conditions, leaving untouched the problem of the material content of knowledge and its agreement with the form of thought; absolute idealism is required to deduce knowledge from the form of mind.

* * *

It was in his renowned course on logic, given at the École Normale Supérieur in 1876–1877, that, for the first time, Lachelier lays out the plan for this new reflexive progress and proclaims that the same movement of turning back on oneself is what brings inquirers to absolute thought in its purity and to God himself who is "thought itself in its absolute power to will and know things." Therefore we are invited to seek in ourselves what we look for in vain outside ourselves and to "find within ourselves, at the base of our consciousness, the substance of our soul, the world's supreme principle."

It is a question therefore of reaching pure thought beyond its determinations, the pure form of reason before it gives itself any matter, the pure form of freedom before it engages in a concrete nature.

The whole problem will be to know whether this intellectual consciousness is in fact a distinct reality from sensory consciousness and whether it does not vanish, volatize when we purify it of its determinations, whether it fades into a "empty frame, a meaningless I'm not sure what, nothingness."

Every assumption favors this intellectual consciousness: it must be real, for the many presupposes the one and the multiple forms of sensory consciousness are all contingent when considered separately; what is more, it can be grasped if we show that it has a precise function in cognition; if it were merely a reproductive function, a means of copying a reality distinct from it, it would not be able to reflect on itself, separate from any contingent act of consciousness; but if it does have a decisive, creative role in the act of cognition, we can grasp this prior to its creations, "apart from its determinations."

This effort will be in vain, a purely verbal trick, to the eye of an impenitent empiricist, for whom the mind is nothing before some act of knowing and knowledge, nothing apart from some concrete input. The idealist, on the contrary, believes that the mind is the author of knowing and knowledge is a universal, preformed map of the absolute.

One understands therefore that reflexive method, in the final analysis, is neither an experience nor pure reasoning but "an intermediary procedure, or rather a higher one, an intellectual intuition, properly speaking."

If it is true that we can grant some consistency to this intellectual intuition, we can affirm that it is God himself we have gotten to in our absolute power to think anything at all. We can be sure of this insofar as we have renounced any ontologism and all transcendence. Skepticism, we know, is the ceaselessly reborn fruit of realism. Just as the reality of the world is assured the moment one states its being internal to the act of cognition, in the same way we remove God from skepticism the moment we look for him within ourselves; if it is true that to exist is to be under the jurisdiction of thought, God is more certain than any other existence: he does not exist but rather makes things exist; he is "the mind's very reality."[1]

* * *

By bringing us to the antipode of skepticism, idealism allows us to realize the dream that this disciple of Maine de Biran nourished beginning in 1868: "to distinguish from oneself, as a second consciousness, what is more internal to us than ourselves . . . the soul of our soul" (letter to Boutroux, September 10, 1868).

The time has come to elucidate the nature of this intellectual consciousness which, at its base, is God himself. What is imposed on us is an indirect verification of the absoluteness of thought, a move back from the absolute to the relative, from God to the world, from an impersonal mind to the many instances of individual sensibilities, a movement whose place in absolute idealism is well-known to us.

* * *

"That mind, reason, freedom are not chimera," and that in their absolute ground they are God himself, is what the article "Psychology and Metaphysics" was meant to demonstrate.

Before anything else, it is necessary to establish the failure of psychological method, of introspection. If we dig deeper into the powers of our nature, if we analyze, using a purely descriptive method, the *facts* of our consciousness, its psychic givens, we never will encounter our mind.

One has always sought to discover too much or too little in man by using psychology. Empiricists see in human nature only a doubling of our nerve impulses and in psychology a provisionally autonomous branch of physiology. Eclectics, on the contrary, believe that, through introspection, they can discover the *fact* of reason, the *fact* of volition, and behind these human facts, the divine *fact*, the divine will, divine reason.

A double error: an empiricist error; for one does not actually see what a pure movement may be, a movement that would not be a fact of consciousness. Hume was wrong: the fact of consciousness is an ungeneratable given.

But no more is Cousin correct: there is not a rational fact; psychology does not lead as far as he believed, and the error of empiricism is precisely the result of the excesses of a metaphysical psychology.

All that psychology can ground is a naturalism which no doubt will be a materialism, but which is also all the more foreign to a true spiritualism. Human nature lives on three levels of increasing depth.

First of all, a superficial life will discover in man only a perceptive system and in it just the basis of seeing and movement. Under this first aspect, sensation reduces to a system of places, limited patches of color, or zones of resistance—if we can see only what appears in space—and the changes in the relations between these patches and zones—if we think about movement.

But a system of relations presupposes contents, limits, some matter to be limited: in short, it is necessary to assume a second level of consciousness where sensation is something filled and alive. Quantity implies quality. Another insight will confirm the introduction of quality: sensation necessarily has two faces. One face when it appears as an object, and another when it is a modification of me. More precisely, by its intensity, tone, and all the other qualitative and affective characters, sensation is in me; through its movement, figure, proportion, and all the other relations, it is an object.

But this is not all: our sensory consciousness is not exhausted in the play of qualities and affects; do we not say that we fight pain or that we abandon ourselves to pleasure? Similarly, in moral matters, do we not say that we take pleasure or find pain? We are therefore other than our affections; there is a "primitive tendency which feeling may stimulate but not create."[2] We are a will.

This is how things are: it suffices undoubtedly to oppose us to Hume's empiricism; but, beyond this, it is Cousin who is wrong: "We know quite well that the blind power which we have described as consciousness is not an intellect and that the spontaneity which we attribute to it has nothing in common with moral liberty. We have not hesitated to admit the fundamental thesis of the new psychology, i.e., the identity of consciousness with physical reality. All we have done is to enlarge this point of view without replacing it and have transformed the materialism which it implicitly professes into a kind of naturalism. Taken by and large, this kind of view is always reasonably true, and spiritualistic views are mistaken."[3]

What are we left with if not precisely that reason is not a fact, a given nature, and that the method that recognizes this is neither descriptive nor empirical? (In a letter to Rauh, from November 10, 1893, he denounces in the expression "rational fact" a kind of intellectual empiricism like that of the Scottish philosophers.)

But how can reason and freedom be something without being givens?

The analysis of the notion of a "given" is going to reveal to us the impotence of this idea as self-sufficient, and the nonsense of giving primacy to what is given. To be given, sensory consciousness presupposes another consciousness, an intellectual consciousness, which differs from it in every way, for it is not something given but something that posits itself.

Here is a new level of existence, which is no longer that of a fact, but of right. What must be shown is that we are not victims of a mirage or some verbal artifact.

How to demonstrate this if not by showing that sensory consciousness would be nothing without the stamp of reason? This indirect proof will be the best way of bringing to light the existence and the role of this intellectual consciousness. This negative method is moreover the only one that is available to us at this time. The ever-so-special nature of this may perhaps require a totally different method for us to deal with it directly and in itself. For the moment, it is possible only to demonstrate its place.

What would the will, feeling, and perception be therefore without this intellectual consciousness? Let us set aside the will, which is not given to us in itself, but through the intermediary of our feelings[4]: it is a feeling of discontent that reveals a need, and this tendency occurs only through "the continuous movement which transforms the need bit by bit into pain and which brings out of this very pain the pleasure that accompanies the satisfaction of need and the sense of well-being which follows it."[5] Being given only as the root of some feeling and the "first condition of every given," the will brings us back to the two real givens: feelings and sensations.

Taken by themselves, do feeling and sensation have the right to say that they are real and true? No: to be an impression and to be knowledge are not the same thing. There is a vast difference separating feeling from judgment, sensory consciousness from intellectual consciousness.

Let us add that the perception of space in its pure state reveals the role of thinking in cognition: the third dimension is not a sensory given; the passage from the surface to the solid is in reality the passage from a spot to the conception of an object: a solid body, a thing is an idea (see the analogous analysis in Lagneau).

So, our description of sensory consciousness brings into play something other than this sensory consciousness: a system of judgment, a science and not a feeling: we have affirmed the truth of feeling; if we did not have this intellectual consciousness, we would not have been able to describe ourselves; we would have felt something but not known something: "The fact is, in the first place, that one can feel without knowing it. . . . But even when we know that we are feeling, our affection and the awareness of it are two quite different things. Our awareness of pain is not painful but true."[6]

In the same way, an astronomical phenomenon is an object of perception; it is just the physical aspect of a unique phenomenon which, through its subjective face, is a sensation. But perception cannot become reflexive consciousness of itself, for without the stamp of our intellectual consciousness, sensation would fade into a dream-like atmosphere. The universe would have the strangeness of a distraction or, better, a kind of psychasthenia. For Pierre Janet, reason is the true function of the real, which assures its consistency with reality.[7] Through it, perception is actually a "true hallucination," if we take up one of Hyppolite Taine's formulations in an unexpected way; it plays the same role in the rhythmic structure of poetry, like the crag-like statement that, according to Paul Valéry, conveys the fleeting impressing of "the object's enduring"; through perception reason makes "a thing, a being which exists in itself, which existed before our perception of it, and which will continue to exist after we shall have ceased to perceive it."[8]

Moving beyond the most modern psychology, which makes the objectivity of perception and the sense of the real a very complex function, and an operation sometimes superior to the automatism of ratiocination, Lachelier places reason at the very root of psychic life. Through it, the world appears as objective: this intellectual consciousness liberates it in combining the thought both of subjectivity and sensory consciousness.[9]

In this way we are freed from our sensory consciousness, and, by placing ourselves outside time and every place, we have posited the absolute truth of a subjective state: we can consider it as future and refer to it as past, precisely because that affirmation we make of this internal state is not part of this internal state. The skeptic, who refuses to go beyond the subjective state of doubt, does so despite himself and affirms the truth of his doubt as absolute. The me that is known is the individual human animal; the knowing me is the absolute subject of cognition. The human animal is thus part of the world, which Lachelier says that it was thinking that does not think about itself, dependent on a thinking that does think about itself. Insofar as we are only sensation, feeling, and even volition, we are bound to the framework of the world. We are this thought that does not think about itself. But insofar as we reach this intellectual consciousness, we become the thinking that thinks its thoughts—that is, God: to pass from feeling to knowing is to pass from the point of view of individuality to that of God. Here the phrase "point of view" is very misleading because every point of view is relative and contingent: science insofar as it is valid is a lawgiver like God.

Knowing posits the true as absolute. The "I think," the form of all forms, the stamp of truth, the highest category of being, is in reality a "God who thinks" and a radically immanent "God who thinks," wholly internal to me; but does it really merit the name "me, formal, impersonal, infinitely distant from my real me, for it is the impalpable and luminous milieu, the intelligible aether in which all this takes place"? (letter to Janet, December 12, 1891).

* * *

We have (in the Kantian sense of justification) "deduced" intellectual consciousness, which is God in us, but we have done so negatively. Therefore we have reached only the border of knowledge; what we must seek is an intellectual intuition in order to unite ourselves to it; for what is true about intellectual consciousness in its relations with sensory knowledge is also true of reflection in its relation to this intellectual consciousness: "Knowing is not an external and mechanical action which one being can force on another. To know something one must in some manner become that very thing, and to accomplish this, one must not in the first instance be other than himself."[10] Reflection must therefore be numerically identical with intellectual consciousness; it must be this intellectual consciousness operating in plain sight, in full awareness of itself. Reflection must consciously redo what reason does spontaneously. That is, reflection must itself become absolute and impersonal thought.

* * *

Yet if reflection is to redo the spontaneous work of reason, it must mime the very process of reason. But, if the nature of this intellectual consciousness is totally different from that of sensory consciousness—that is, reflection— reflection too, must take a wholly new direction. Reason is opposed to sensory consciousness as something *de jure* to something *de facto*. Reason assures the genuine being of the contents of sensory consciousness; being is more than an instance of concrete existence; it goes beyond past and future and timelessly posits the existence that the present, past, and future actually realize.

Reason posits the validity of being, that it deserves to exist in some time and place. What "is," is "that which *one must* perceive and feel in virtue of the laws of nature and of consciousness."[11]

So, we catch sight of the true nature of reason: "How, though, are we to know that we ought feel or to perceive one thing rather than another?" How else than because there is "prior to all experience, an idea of what must be, an ideal being as Plato would have it, which may function for us as the type and measure of real being"?[12]

So what Lachelier brings us to is a form of Platonism: a post-Kantian Platonism we might call it, but a genuine Platonism: a philosophy that wants to make the concrete an indication of the abstract, that conceives of the abstract as true being, a philosophy for which the absolute science is not of what is concrete but of what is abstract, which consists in finding in the articulation of "the measure and type" of concrete relations—this philosophy is a Platonism.

As a result, the philosopher's program will be to construct this science which, if it were to constitute itself, would be "both a science of thought and of all things."[13] Reflection therefore is the passage from appearing to being. The world of phenomena cannot, by itself, know itself as phenomenal. It requires the doubling of intellectual consciousness. It should be noted that this passage from appearance to being has nothing to do with creation. It is rather the *prise de conscience* of an implicit existence. The skeptic himself, who thinks his doubt, makes use of this intellectual consciousness; there is no need to demonstrate the existence of this consciousness to him, but simply to make him aware of it, by showing him that without it, he would not be able to know that he doubts. The passage from appearance to being therefore does not create anything; it is just a passage from the implicit to the explicit.

But this is a very modern Platonism: in a letter to Rauh (1893)—the same letter in which he declares reason to be a thing in itself—Lachelier hastens to add that his Platonism is to be interpreted in an anti-substantialist sense (letter to Rauh, 1893). This is an important assertion, one that will not yet take on its full meaning if we content ourselves with purely and simply reintegrating the thing-in-itself into the subject; an integral anti-substantialism must renounce treating reason as a thing; the absolute me is not a me-substance for it would be a thing only in virtue of some other thought, which would confer on it the dignity of existence and of truth; furthermore, the world of ideas would be juxtaposed to the concrete world as one thing alongside another thing. The "I think" would be external to consciousness, and the relation of knowing would collapse into a material operation of a mechanical and spatial kind.[14] This intellectual consciousness is not a thing, but a value, an absolute right to exist.

So the study of pure thinking must be of a wholly special nature: it must not treat reason as an object and consequently must not distinguish itself, as a consciousness of a subject distinguishes itself from a consciousness of an object.

As Kant puts it, the "I think"—and, speaking like an absolute idealist, the "God thinks"—can never be an object; it is uniquely the pure subject.

How then to avoid reflection objectifying, substantifying the pure me? Only on one condition: metaphysics must stop being a higher form of empiricism, reflection must identify itself with the very movement of thought by which the subject produces itself, philosophy must plainly mimic the generation of the being of thinking.

> The idea which we must use for judging everything which is given us cannot be one of the things that is given. Unless, then, this idea produces itself in us, does there remain anything other than the possibility that it is a living dialectic—as we ourselves are so far as we are intelligible subjects? Let us not be afraid somehow to suspend thought in the void, for it can be grounded only on itself and everything else can be based only upon it. . . . The last of these elements, pure thought, is an idea which is produced of itself and whose real nature we are unable to grasp except by *reproducing* it by a process of *a priori* construction or synthesis. This movement from analysis to synthesis is at the same time a movement from psychology to metaphysics.[15]

A supreme and necessarily audacious assertion: audacious for it means saying that we are God insofar as we are capable of renewing the original bonds between ideas, of re-engendering being. It will be necessary to say we are not in time, even though our dialectic unfolds in time; it will be necessary to say that this construction is impersonal, although any philosophy is a human art.

But also a necessary audacity, for a divorce, an inner dissension runs through thinking: unendingly it divides into a lived spontaneity and a reflexive curiosity, whose reconciliation is difficult to conceive.

Let us consider the spontaneity of sensory consciousness, a radical tendency that works obscurely and more or less correctly to compose the harmonious face of the world. But I can affirm this only to the extent that I have detached myself from it, as though I were alien to it, like an impartial spectator. Does the same thing not apply to reason?

I am irremediably double: I have the property of "regarding myself in passing."[16] But this spectator himself acts, to the degree that he exercises his curiosity about the person he is observing. This intellectual consciousness is once again a spontaneity that a new reflection will be able to observe from the outside. Here is a vertigo in which thinking threatens being swallowed up in a sterile, infinite regression: reflection and prospection pursue each other in a ceaselessly renewed race: I unendingly oppose myself to myself, like an observer who becomes a problem for another observer. And so on and so on.

If we look more closely, this divorce within thinking is the very drama of idealism: idealism tries to absorb everything into the act of a pure subject. But to the degree that idealism is reflection, it always leaves an ultimate perspective outside itself, which is the very act of its own reflection, which proposes itself as another object to be reabsorbed into the subject.

This undoubtedly is the profound meaning of the final audacity of Lachelier's philosophy: it comes down to reflection's identifying itself with the fundamental prospection of the life of the mind, a prospection carried out by every thought, but without its being aware of it. Philosophy only adds to this consciousness of it. It retraces in plain light the path that every thought implicitly traces. Ceasing to be a sterile turning back on the self, ceasing to always situate itself after the act like a neutral arbitrator, ceasing to decompose, to analyze acts after the fact, and to be the science of resolved problems, reflection is going to try to be itself the resolution of these problems, but a resolution aware of itself.

We will be assured of succeeding only if the ideas created by the mind's spontaneity can justify themselves—not some new idea, in other words if the problem raised by reflection is justified by the exploration of reflection itself. For example, the idea of truth posed by this spontaneity is judged by the reflection that asks for its justification: but this judgment, this doubt about the idea of truth, brings into play the mind's spontaneity. This active doubt once again envelops the idea of truth. In this way, prospection and reflection adhere to each other.

But two difficulties await us: first of all, how to avoid encountering, under the name of intellectual consciousness, an empty form, a nothing, a power of affirmation about which in the end we can affirm nothing. Kant's slipperiness here is well known. Having affirmed that the sensible is affirmable only by an act of the understanding, he substitutes a table of concepts for the faculty of judgment: this ultimate ransom Kant pays to Aristotelianism will weigh heavily on the whole course of post-Kantian philosophy.

* * *

It is, undoubtedly, at this price that the "I think" takes on some consistency, for it is in itself perfectly undetermined: Descartes, first, had substituted for the *cogito*—which can be only an act, a verb—the enumeration of *cogitata*, of the objects of thought, concepts.

It is the tragic fate of idealism to posit, on the one hand, the primacy of the act of thinking over the material thing and even over the thinking thing, and, on the other hand, being unable to avoid confusion and vagueness by surreptitiously substituting a philosophy of the concept for a philosophy of judgment—in short, by substituting intellectual things for the intellect. This realism, however insidious, of the thought-thing always menaces any study of thinking.

Faced with this difficulty, Lachelier rightly saw that a dialectic of thinking must be a process of purification, a reconquering of the power of judging over its conceptual incarnations.

Lachelier's dialectic is not a game of concepts, but a liberating of the concept, a supreme effort by the mind to transcend its dogmas and concepts.

Lagneau, too, will discover this implicit doubling within every affirmation, and, fearing having to substantialize this "soul of affirmation," will observe a radical agnosticism when it comes to absolute thought, preferring to say what it is not rather than what it is. He will content himself with affirming that one cannot deny it without contradiction, nor can one affirm it without betraying it. Lagneau always prefers the way of doubt to that of a positive conquest, the way of negation to that of a dialectic.

A second difficulty awaits us: the ascending dialectic tries to re-engender being, but it is also necessary to take the reverse path, to show how this spontaneity of spirit creates every meaningful operation along the way. This is a formidable difficulty for idealism: the ransom for a philosophy of the absolute is the genesis of the finite. The sensible world is opposed to the ideal world like the *de facto* to the *de jure*. It will come down to knowing how to descend again from the *de jure* to the *de facto*. Ideal *being*[17] is the type and the measure of real *being*: but if it is impossible to recognize the model in the copy, there is no passage from the copy to the model, and there is no reason, it seems, for absolute thought to project itself on planes as opaque as those of the will and of affection. Starting here, we sense the capital role that the notion of a symbol will play in this descending dialectic that reconnects facts and right.

There is more: will the given reattached to the right rediscover the spontaneity of reason? Or must it not first be, through another presentation, that the fact should be given after it has been reconnected to the right? This nuance is important, for it will be a question of knowing whether spontaneity can engender sensory life or whether it depends on a later unification unable to fill a profound dualism, that of mind and nature.

* * *

The time has come to attempt this genesis of thought through the fusion of intellectual spontaneity and reflection.

Our starting point will be the idea of truth: Why? Because the idea of truth is encompassed in the very doubt we can have about it and that manifests the unity of reflection and the spontaneity of thinking: if I try to consider the idea of being as an object, distinct from the act that posits it, to judge it, I perceive that I judge the idea of being only in light of this very same idea. The idea is therefore both the act and the content of the supreme act of thinking. "Need one ask that the idea of being regarded as the form of thought should have to be guaranteed in its turn by a prior form? No doubt it does, and it is just this which takes place. For this idea, whose existence is not being inquired into, is brought by this very process to the level of an object of thought. This new object of thought immediately finds its guarantee in a new form, since whether it exists or does not exist, it still *is true* either that it exists or does not exist. The idea of being then is deduced from itself not merely once but as often as one wishes, or *ad infinitum*. It produces and guarantees itself absolutely."[18] But are we really face-to-face with the absolute spontaneity of thinking? No: we do not have two functions of one idea here. that of a form-function and that of an object-function: "The idea of being regarded as the form of this very thought has as its antecedent and guarantee the idea of being regarded as the form of this very thought."[19]

We cannot therefore truly speak of a spontaneity of spirit, which must be an act, the copula of a judgment, as Brunschvicg has demonstrated in his *Modalité du Judgment*. Two concepts, not two acts, are what translate the double aspect of the idea of truth in its auto-production: "Being is. Contrary to the usual interpretation we move in this proposition from the attribute to the subject. For thought begins by establishing its proper form which is being as attribute, but an attribute can always be taken as the subject of itself; and, to anything that is, even to non-being, we may attribute the notion of being. Thus, being is."[20] This text shows that it is impossible to interpret this first form of being any way other than as an idea, a concept. But then we are not dealing with the spontaneity of thought, which is an act, which works as the copula, and not as the subject or an attribute.

Will someone say that Lachelier, like Kant, has slipped from a philosophy of judgment to a philosophy of the concept? There remains a second solution: the very one I outlined above, in indicating the first difficulty of the dialectic: across those three phases the absolute subject is perhaps not always at the same degree of purity; pure spirit, which is an act, first loses itself in the concept, beginning from below itself, regaining itself through the dialectic to reattain its purity only at the third step. Therefore we must not look for the absolute spontaneity of thinking in the first two steps, but only at the end of the dialectic.

This point of view will be fully justified if we envisage the meaning of the third step of the dialectic. Having posited the idea of abstract being, then of concrete being, the dialectic posits the act of affirmation, which is expressed precisely by the copula of a judgment. This power of affirmation is the true absolute spontaneity of spirit, an act, not an idea. Hence the first and second steps in the dialectic do not allow putting ourselves face-to-face with an absolute subject, but with its works, concepts, ideas, forms, objects of reflection.

We came upon the first difficulty, now we are going to meet the second one; this idea of reflection must "explain two elements of sensible consciousness: that by reason of which it can in some manner reflect upon itself, and that on which it confers by this (reflective) process an objective value."[21]

If we envisage that the idea of being, in justifying itself, leads to infinity, we realize that this auto-production serves as both "measure and type," both time and the line on which we see an instant and a point ceaselessly precede itself.

Here is where we come to the notion of symbol, which serves as a bridge between the absolute and the relative, between intellectual and sensible consciousness, between God and the world.

But it is important that we pose the question: does this come down to a generation of sensible consciousness or is it an after-the-fact justification that has nothing to do with the origin, but that first assumes the sensible element be given? The second hypothesis seems the truer one: indeed, if Lachelier talks about "reconstructing the living consciousness,"[22] he means by this reconstruction the meaning made clear in the previous pages:

"Evidently there really exists in us an intellectual consciousness which adds nothing to the content of the sensible consciousness, but which stamps this content with the seal of objectivity."[23] If it adds nothing, is this not because it presupposes what it does not add: movement and desire are not solicited by intellectual consciousness, but the synthesis is based on what is given for analysis. The analysis proposes its conclusions as a hypothesis; the synthesis justifies them but does not discover them. The study of the symbol shows clearly that the synthesis is not substituted for the analysis but prolongs it. The analysis proposes the givens; the synthesis validates them. "Thus we succeed in reconstructing the living consciousness as analysis had given it to us. We know now that it has no less objective value than the abstract and mechanical consciousness which we have previously constructed."[24]

Yet, this proceeding through a symbol is extremely arbitrary. Before discovering that the line is a symbol of the deduction of the idea of being, it was necessary surreptitiously to introduce space into the schema of this deduction; it was necessary to consider ideas as external to one another for the deduction to be able to symbolize the points of a line as something external. Does this make sense? We may well doubt it. In any case, if this exteriority of the moments of thought makes any sense, it will be sufficient to prove that we are not face-to-face with the spontaneity of the spirit, which is wholly internal, but with disjoint concepts.

Finally, Lachelier envisages a reaction of the idea of being on its symbol: logical necessity becomes mechanical necessity. One look is enough to rediscover in this first stage of the deduction the first movement of the *Foundations of Induction*: abstract, mechanical consciousness. But rather than the abstract necessity of human thinking and the mechanical necessity of the sensory world's being posed as riddles, and their reciprocal fitting together as a mystery, mind is grounded in God and sensory consciousness in spirit.

* * *

It is as well the second philosophy of the *Foundations of Induction* that we rediscover along with the second dialectical stage—but as equally deified. This second philosophy is constructed like the first one: an idea is posed by the dialectical movement, it gets expressed in a sensible symbol, and the symbol reacts back on the idea. This idea this time is the subject of existence, essence, the plentitude of being; the first idea was only the framework of existence, the property of existing, the possible attribute of a being. Now we discover "not the fact of being but *that which it is*."[25]

What is the sensible symbol of this ideal being? We will note that concrete being no longer is "external to but internal to itself."[26] Its immediate symbol therefore is not extensive: it is a sensation. A second symbol is enclosed within the first one: according to Leibniz, sensation is not simple but includes a multiplicity of tiny perceptions. The symbol of this simultaneous multiplicity is a two-dimensional space, the surface, which we have already seen; it is concrete space.

Finally, from the contact of these two sensible symbols, "desire, sensation, and visible extension form parts of consciousness and are the very elements of nature."[27]

At first glance, it seems that with this second dialectical degree we should finally meet living thought and not a conceptual construction: "However, thought does tend of its own accord to go beyond the sphere of the abstract and the empty. Thought spontaneously proposes the concrete being in order to thus become concrete and living thought."[28]

* * *

And yet, we still have here only an idea and not a spontaneity, an act. It is not because we pass from abstract being to concrete being that we leave behind the conceptual sphere. We have simply passed from the abstract to the concrete idea. In fact, Lachelier himself has told us this: dialectic engenders only ideal being, the measure and type of concrete existence. With an ideal being we do not reach the spontaneity of nature, and to the degree that this being is an idea, neither do we do enter the spontaneity of thinking, but rather we have an idea of the distinct reflection of the act that posits it.

Is it not still only in a concept that this second time of the dialectic expresses itself? "We repeat for the second time: Being is. Now we intend to move in the customary manner from the subject to the attribute in this proposition. In the first place, being is presented in itself, as subject and essence. In the second place, it *is* manifested outside of itself by the attribute of existence."[29]

This is a decisive proof of our interpretation; this second idea of being will be judged by the third one as a distinct consciousness of itself. What might this mean if not that we are once again face-to-face with an object and not a pure subject?

The passage from the first to the second degree of reflection still has to be analyzed: a capital idea, introduced in the *Foundations of Induction*, is that there is no logical connection between these two ideas of being.

No doubt, the second one appears as "the complement" of the first one; we may even say that "it completes and justifies it."[30] But, in reality, it is the second idea of being that is the first and fundamental one. A truly perfect spirit would go immediately to the will and see only in necessity a residue of finality. This reversal of priority seems implied in the following lines: "Abstract being attaches itself to concrete being as though to its root; we cannot even conceive of existence except as some kind of manifestation of that which exists."[31] Does not the word *manifestation* permit us to say that the first idea of being is a symbol of the second one? Comparing the text from *Psychology and Metaphysics* with the similar text from *Foundations of Induction* seems to authorize this interpretation. "The real reasons for things are ends which, regarded as forms, constitute things themselves. Matter and causes are a necessary hypothesis or rather an indispensable *symbol* through which we project into time and space that which is itself superior to both. The opposition of the concrete to the abstract, of finality to mechanism, is grounded only on the distinction of our faculties. Thought which would renounce itself in order to lose itself, or rather in order to find itself entirely in the object, would come to know no other law than that of harmony and no other light than beauty."[32]

But if this is so, we are justified in interpreting synthesis as an effort to dig deeply, a passage from appearance to being internal to absolute thought, a production of the light that convicts every prior clarification of obscurity. "Purpose, sensation, and the surface are more true than causality, empty time, and the line, because all three correspond to a higher form and, so to speak, to the second power of the power of being."[33]

In any case, let us retain this affirmation that the idea of concrete being is in its own way a first idea, an absolute starting point. But by what right, then, can we posit concrete being? If we want the form of an act to be adequate to its content, the will must be posited voluntarily, just as necessity is posited necessarily. This was how Lachelier had already passed from mechanism to finality in *Foundations of Induction*.

That this second idea of being still remains very abstract cannot be doubted; still Lachelier's plan is to break through the mechanical framework of thought and to subordinate it to the full aspiration and the tendency, the impulse toward the Good, concerning which he says to Janet: "If there is something rational, without a doubt there is something in it of the real, the living, the good and the fortunate, and that not everything comes down to logic and pure indifference. Being is better than nothing, said Bossuet" (letter to Janet, December 12, 1891).

* * *

A new reflective effort forces us to affirm that concrete being still differs from the fecundity of thinking: concrete being can once again return to the rank of an object and pass through the screen of a distinct consciousness of it, "which would become in some fashion the witness of its truth and the judge of its right to be."³⁴

What, therefore, is this consciousness, if not the very soul of affirmation, the pure power to judge? The epitome of being "is to be superior to every nature and freed from every essence. This is to be nothing other than itself, so to speak, that is to say, to be the pure consciousness and pure affirmation of itself."³⁵

We come to the end of our inquiry: to God himself, the soul of our soul, pure thinking apart from any of its determinations. If we want to speak using logical terms, we will say that this pure thought, which animates every thought, is the copula of judgment, "which asserts the attribute of the subject and makes the proposition pass wholly from potency to act."³⁶ "We shall find no difficulty in establishing the objective value of this third idea, for if concrete being has already seemed to us as more true than abstract being, how much more true will be the idea which completes the truth of both the first and second ideas of being and which is truth and light itself."³⁷

So everything that remains holds only owing to this third potentiality of being; without it, the truth of the first two would have remained "virtual and latent." We have definitively passed from appearance to being. It was not true that the first idea was the whole truth; it was only the idea of truth, a product of thinking and its most impoverished one; only the third idea is the truth itself, but not as a form or an idea, but the truth itself, that is, the act of truth: to pass from appearance to being, therefore is also to pass from the product to its production, from the concept to the judgment.

Nor is it true that the second idea was alive and alight; it was only the idea of life, life crystallized into a concept. The third potentiality of being is the light, the act of illumination.

Therefore it is only at this stage that the "absolute spontaneity of spirit" is fulfilled in the adequation of spiritual action and reflection. The first forms of being were still nature, essence, object, a rational fact.

It would be wrong to believe that the dialectic is pure spirit which unfolds on the same level, in three equivalent phases, for pure spirit realizes itself and fulfills itself (which is the same thing) only at the third level; at the third stage alone does it affirm itself—that is, as both pure act and pure consciousness at one and the same time, prospection, and reflection. Pure spirit therefore starts, in a way, short of itself, from detached, conceptual secondary products. Lachelier's dialectic is a search for judgment, the pure act starting from concepts, ideas, objects. The first two stages were only *cogitata*: the third stage alone is the *cogito*, or rather *Deus cogitat*.

In the same way, Lagneau will say that the highest form of existence is beyond nature and that philosophy consists in freeing oneself from nature, by beginning with thought.

Interpreted in this way, Lachelier's synthesis is radically different from that of the post-Kantians, for it is not a rhythmic genesis of concepts but the search for the pure affirmation at the heart of what is affirmable.

Would it be inexact to say that Lachelier's synthesis is in reality a disguised analysis? But there the way taken is regressive, because finality is posited as the support for mechanism, and pure intellectual action then grounds concrete being "by which being is seen and is made to be."[38]

* * *

If analysis is looking for the condition in the conditioned, the dialectic of *Psychology and Metaphysics* is genuinely an analysis. This analysis remains a synthesis because the passage from the conditioned to the condition is absolutely free and each term is sufficient in its own way. But, in this sense, the passage from the first to the second philosophy of the *Foundations of Induction* was already virtually a synthesis. For instance, to the degree that the *Foundations of Induction* contains a synthesis and *Psychology and Metaphysics* an analysis, there is no opposition between the basic method found in each of them.

The sole difference is that the synthesis of *Foundations of Induction* was problematic and not completed. Problematic, because mechanism and finality were posited as human structures and not as absolute forms of thought. Incomplete because the soul of these structures was not uncovered and precisely constituted the enigma of Kantianism; in absolutizing these two forms of thought, Lachelier implicitly posits a third term in his dialectic which is precisely the absolute, which makes them be a structure of thinking. In this sense, the third term was implicitly present in the other two; it was necessary only to become conscious of it. We may even say that the final term is the reason behind the two preceding ones, that the fullness that comes at the end of the effort is the reason for the effort. The real connection between the three terms is the third term: "How can one pass by reasoning from a simple form of consciousness to another form, which, by hypothesis, is not contained in the former? This is just what we have attempted to do in supposing that consciousness and all that it includes gravitates in some fashion toward liberty and intelligence."[39] In this sense, the dialectic is not arbitrary, it is not absolutely discontinuous: it is the search for the absolute as absolute: "This third consciousness is the last; the movement of thought comes to a halt after being sought in necessity, as in its shadow, then in the will, as in its body, being found finally in freedom."[40]

* * *

But someone may say, if the pure act is impersonal, must we not say that reflection distinguishes itself from it, because philosophy remains the work of a human being? Yes and no. No, in the sense that a philosophy claims to make a truth claim, and in so doing, impersonality. A pure philosophy would be a "God thinks." In a pure philosophy, reflection is strictly adequate to the absolute spontaneity of thought. In a discussion at the Philosophy Society, Lachelier says to Gustave Belot: "Nothing is more personal than philosophy, nothing more impersonal when it is a question of validity, since it is total reality; that is, at bottom, if one truly understands things, it is universal reason becoming conscious of itself and giving an account of itself."[41]

However, some distinction is possible between human thought and divine thought, in the sense that human thought is necessarily bound to a sensible matter. (Here is where a third plane of thinking will be inserted: see Chapter 3.) The absolute potentiality of thought is nourished by the content of each individual consciousness; we can say that in man, reason thinks as the sensible consciousness. It is therefore in some way distinct from God through its content, not through its form. The notion of "symbol" is what best accounts for the relations of human reason to God. We are "the people of God," "in the image of God," says the Bible. Pure thought—God—therefore has in us a symbol, not sensible this time, but wholly spiritual, which is personal thought, "applied or empirical thought which reflects upon sensible consciousness and affirms the existence of the elements which constitute it."[42] This thinking is not, in truth, philosophical thinking which is a second-degree thought; this direct thought is an operative thinking, applied to things, inserted into the concrete: it thinks the world before turning back on itself to think itself. Thus, in thinking extended objects, it confers upon them the third dimension, which, we know, is not a sensible given.

We may compare this idea to Spinoza's conception, for which the soul is the idea of the body. Does not Lachelier say that through it "each of us affirms his own life and his own duration and distinguishes these two in affirming them"?[43]

It is by a folding back on itself that our thinking becomes "rational or philosophic knowledge of ourselves and of the world."[44] Or rather, it is through an implicit action of this absolute, which grasps itself in its human symbol: it is the presence of the model in each symbol that guarantees the unity of spirits: "It is the one and single reason, as Cousin believed, which however impersonal it is in itself becomes reflected and personal in us."[45]

As regards God, this is our actual unity and apparent distance. This inwardness of God suffices to definitively oppose the life of spirit to every empiricist image or romantic effusion.

Our true freedom, symbolic of divine freedom, no longer has anything in common with the arbitrariness of desire and the contingency of forces; in the moment, it breaks with the necessity of any moment: "That which is, properly spiritual, is the intellectual, as Bossuet remarked."[46]

Still more forcefully, in a letter to Rauh (February 13, 1893): "Freedom is totally different from our fragile power to choose between good and evil. . . . It is the being of the copula, the form of the proposition, of truth in general."

But, in fact, not every human being has arrived at the same stage: some only affirm themselves as mechanical nerve processes or as a will to live; as they affirm themselves, so they are, for our being is in our consciousness. Therefore they are not really free, nor fully rational. The richness of our life is proportional to the depth of our reflection. Spinoza, whom Lachelier did not know well, had already said, in his dialectic of the three souls, that we are individuals only if we know ourselves to be individuals—the result of our movements, if we know our dependence on the general laws of the universe—and finally free, if we realize in ourselves that divine necessity that depends only on itself; like this, Lachelier will say:

> The act by which we affirm our own being wholly constitutes that being, for it is the very act which is realized and fixed in our character and which is manifested and developed in our history. Hence it must not be said that we affirm ourselves to be such as we are; but on the contrary we are that which we affirm ourselves to be. It especially must not be granted that our present depends upon our past which is no longer in our power, for we create every instant of our life by the single self-same act which at one and the same time is present to each and superior to all. We are conscious of this act and consequently of our liberty in every instant. On the other hand, when we consider these instants in relation to each other we find that they form a continuous chain and an inflexible mechanism. In a word, we achieve a destiny when we choose, or rather we never cease from choosing.[47]

* * *

This is the philosophical God: we can relate this study to three things: 1. An integral rational spiritualism; 2. A doctrine of radical immanence; and 3. An effort to reabsorb the world into pure thought.

Under the first heading, Lachelier's spiritualism is incorporeal and desubstantialized in a way that is difficult to imagine: God's freedom is the being of the copula; what is properly spiritual is intellectual. Under the second heading, the interiority of God to human reason is pushed as far as possible: God is not distinct from the procedure through which we apprehend him; God is the spirit that finds itself in us. Our true freedom is divine freedom, and our true reason divine reason.

* * *

The ultimate foundation of every doctrine of transcendence lies within the heterogeneity of persons. Yet the notion of a person plays no role in Lachelier's philosophy. On the human level, there is no middle term between the individuality of the human animal and the impersonality of truth: in the same letter to Rauh, which we cited above, Lachelier indicates that this middle term of the person would compromise all the objectivity of idealism: "which hangs our spirit on truth. . . . The individual voluntarily thinks but does not create what there is that is true, intellectual in this thinking, but which rather makes him a participant in thought, which was prior to him, and which has no need of his action to subsist, or of the personal form it receives, or of making thought rest on an act that in itself would not be pure logic and pure illumination, that is a leftover substantialism" (February 13, 1893).

The dominant idea of Lachelier's thought—the one that perhaps serves as the basis of all his discussion and every meditation—is that thinking, being free, and in general acting in the deepest sense of the word, do not properly belong to the person and do not necessarily require a personal time, but are *de jure* impersonal. "Freedom," he also tells Rauh, "is totally different from our fragile power to choose between good and evil. . . . It is an idea, or form of freedom, an essential element of thinking or of truth considered apart from every individual existence, in its absolute universality and impersonality."

More clearly still, in his discussion of Boutroux's theses, he ties the doctrine of immanence to that of the impersonality of immanence: "I would hesitate to say, with Le Roy, except where this would be a kind of symbolism, that God is a person, who produces the world through a personal act of his will, or that our life in him will be a continuation of our personal existence. A person is undoubtedly above all else an intelligence, but an intelligence is not necessarily a person and cannot, if we reduce it to what is most essential to it, be one. A person is an intelligence united to a sensibility and cannot, as a result of this, think and act except by following the law of time. But this law, according to Kant, is independent and must make us free."[48]

The only transcendence is not between us and God but between our reason which is God and our animal me. But—and this is the third characteristic of Lachelier's philosophy—this distance is relatively filled if we understand that sensible elements can symbolize their unity, that of reason and freedom. It is even our task in this world to imitate God through the harmony and unity of these elements or of nature.

It is this connection through symbols that connects nature and thought and that completes idealism. Lachelier writes much later, in the notes to the *Dictionnaire Philosophique*: "Philosophy is essentially the science of the subject and is only interested in the object as regards what it finds there concerning the subject."[49]

Lachelier's philosophy strives to renounce neither the purity of spirit nor the latent spirituality of the world: this is what makes his philosophy similar to that of Lagneau and opposes it to that of Brunschvicg. The following chapter will show how he distances himself from Brunschvicg in order to come closer to Lagneau. We may even ask whether it is not from Ravaisson that he draws this double ambition. Regarding the article titled "Spiritualism" in the *Dictionnaire Philosophique*, he writes:

> In a general sense, every doctrine which recognizes the independence and priority of spirit, that is, of conscious thought, may be called *spiritualism*. There is a kind of spiritualism of the first degree which consists merely in placing spirit above nature without clarifying the relationship between the two. But there is a deeper and more complete spiritualism which consists in seeking in the explanation of nature itself within spirit, in believing that the unconscious thought which works in nature is the very same which becomes conscious in man and that it operates only in order to become able to produce an organism which will permit it to pass (by means of the representation of space) from the unconscious to the conscious form.[50]

And again: "Nature is pregnant with spirit."[51]

He writes to Maximilien Winter, in 1892: "Reason comprehends being, even regarding what is irrational about it."

The Living God

A. Philosophy and Faith

It is often said that the true atheist is someone who has no need of God, someone whose knowledge is closed in on itself, fully complete, someone who never runs into radical distress which is the real place for God, what thought and action lacks, which is the negative sign and an appeal for a Presence.

Let us apply this idea to Lachelier's religious faith. What role will faith play in such a philosophy? Or, rather, what need may we have for faith? Was not everything achieved with the intellectual intuition of pure reason and the reassuring vision of nature's symbolism? Yet as Lachelier himself has taught us, all progress in thinking is not a complement to, a supererogatory ornament, a flash at the peak of an edifice—rather, each new initiative of reflection picks up the whole base, rediscovers darkness where one believes one sees light. The final term of the dialectic is conceived as the ultimate term that cannot be surpassed or surmounted.

Do we have any need for faith in these conditions? This is the real question that must now occupy us; if it is true that every problem of presence is first a problem of absence, we can ask what it is that philosophy *lacks*.

* * *

What the philosophical knowledge of God lacks is not truth, but richness and fullness.

God, let it not be forgotten, for the philosopher is the being of the copula, a pure form, an empty framework, the soul of thinking beyond all its determinations. Must we not admit that for us this principle of every determination is just a total indetermination, that this source of plenitude for us is our poverty? "Perhaps the act of knowing, as it is accomplished in us, although free, and even the only form we know of freedom, does not for all that exhaust the essence of freedom; perhaps, in other words, God is not at bottom wholly in us, but only a reflection, an idea, as light but not as power."

Therefore we have only an incomplete idea of pure reason, of God: not a false idea but an incomplete one, for the essence of freedom "is essentially to be what comes last, or rather first." Formal freedom is not something beyond: it is God. Therefore it is not an endpoint to be surpassed but a frame that must be filled. The sole flaw of this freedom is that it is formal and not material: "What I have noted, in reading Kant, is that we are only aware of a formal infinity, or thought, and that material infinity or existence is just as foreign to our consciousness as it is distinct from the universe." This is what he wrote to Ravaisson in 1868.

Let us look again at this old letter to Ravaisson: "Does consciousness of our freedom only give us the idea of an absolute in general, which we will be incapable of determining, or that we have only a really undetermined and chimerical reason to believe, were a revelation properly speaking not to have taught us that the substance of this absolute is love [*la charité*]?" (May 4, 1871).

The passage from the philosophical God to the Christian God, from the God who is only the copula of judgment to the God who is love, this is the final problem of Lachelier's philosophy.

But what does this freedom which is not merely formal, but material, mean? It can have only one meaning, one which leads us to two propositions: 1. Every determination comes from the union of matter and a form; freedom becomes actual only if it is determined and materially formal; 2. But freedom as we conceive it gets determined only through betraying itself: in the order that is the only one accessible to us here below, there is no matter adequate to the pure form of freedom. This state, in which reason would receive a content proportioned to it, is properly what is the beyond. It is what the object of faith is and what constitutes true transcendence.

1. That for Lachelier reason is a form that necessarily calls for matter is what several texts allow us to establish: regarding the article "Matter" in the *Dictionnaire Philosophique*, Lachelier writes:

> I believe one cannot really take up the meaning of the words matter and materialism other than by starting from Aristotle. It seems clear

to me that, in every being, there are (1) what gives it its meaning and interest: its idea or form; (2) what for this form is a necessary ground, apart from which it would be abstract or merely possible.... Except that I would not say with Ravaisson that in ascending, or rather descending, in this sense, one ends up not being able to find anything more: I think there is a real end, what Leibniz considered rightly an indispensable element of his monad, a principle of resistance, or delayed action, without which any effort would be lost in the void or rather not really ever begin; and in a general way, in returning the other way, we will discover that there must always be matter for a form, facts, for example, for any systematic construction, normative tendencies, sufficiently energetic for virtue, a sufficient degree of concrete beauty that can serve as the basis for the beauty of their expression.[1]

Therefore there is an ideal to reason, which Lachelier, following Kant, calls *Intuition*, where the object, the content of thought, would be exactly adequate to its form: "Everything that is an object of thought is other than the act of thinking, and thinking cannot draw this from itself; but this is because thinking is not what it means to be or ought to be, that is, to be intuitive, for if it were intuitive its object would not be external to it, but immanent, or rather the two together would be one and the same idea, or truth."[2] This is a crucial text: it follows that intuition corresponds exactly to the idea of a freedom that would be both pure form and pure matter.

2. But, precisely, we possess only the form of this reason; we do not know it as having an adequate content: as soon as it receives a determination, it receives matter that is disproportionate to it. Indeed, the form of judgment applies to an improper matter, a sensible content: "No one was more unpitying about this than Kant," he writes in the article on "Reason," "when it comes to our aspiration for purely intellectual knowledge about the ground of things; no one did more to make this irresistible, by demonstrating that this knowledge is the only knowledge worthy of the name, sensible knowledge is not to no avail—for it is symbolic of true knowledge, and we do grasp being *per speculum* and *in enigmate*—but it is inadequate, provisory, and entirely to no avail when it believes it can grasp reality in what is sensible."[3] We are therefore driven to a strange contradiction, which is the very instability of our nature. We require a real complement to the form of reason, but we find it nowhere:

And yet, the determined complement (extensively and intensively), the explained complement (in terms of becoming and existence), *must be*, for we cannot prevent ourselves from seeking it; but we must look for it beyond time and space, that is, there where it is currently impossible for us to find it. Whence the paradox in Kant's language that the *intelligible*, that is, the proper object of our reasoning, is precisely what depends on everything our reasoning can grasp.... Kant always clung to his sober and severe conception of a purely symbolic knowledge through the sensible. But one sees why his successors should have dreamt of a direct and adequate knowledge of the real, with no basis in the sensible; because of this, for them, that new role for Reason, becomes not only a positing, an affirmation, but an intuition of the real entirely identified with it.[4]

* * *

These texts, I believe, are the real introduction of faith, for they demonstrate its place. It still remains to show that faith implies these affirmations, which philosophy is no longer competent to deal with, and that faith is the hope of a content adequate to our reason; then we have to ask what grounds we can draw from for this content of faith.

Regarding Lachelier's religious thought, we have some valuable pages to guide us: his *Notes on Pascal's Wager* from 1901, and some interventions at the French Philosophy Society, including his lively discussion with Boutroux regarding his theses: "Science and Religion" (on November 19, 1908).

What is the content of religion? "It is the idea ... of an external existence higher than nature, or of what I will call a beyond. It is this beyond that today every religious soul addresses, faith and love."[5]

If we take this further, we recognize in it all the features of pure reason which gives its content to itself:

> Is it therefore in the image of our thought that we can represent this beyond to ourselves? Yes and no: yes, in the sense that it is distinguished from nature and posits itself for our thinking; no in the sense that it is not within us at least presently a complete being, but a mere form for which nature provides the content, and which does not itself have, outside of nature, either life or reality. But there is one thing we can at least admit without understanding it: the existence of a thought that would not have need, as we do, of an empirical content, but which would give itself to itself, or rather which would be for itself a content of another order, and which would be consequently for itself what our reason cannot be except in union with nature: a complete, real, and living being.[6]

This is precisely what we call eternal life. It would be a mistake to see any attachment to my animal me "a kind of natural revenge against death."[7] Eternal life is our fusion with this complete being, with the living God.

Now, having assured ourselves that we have not overlooked faith's true content, the moment has come to evaluate its value; but in doing so we are evaluating a new knowledge based upon our older knowledge. Whether we want to or not, to evaluate faith is to judge it philosophically. If by definition, faith cannot be demonstrated, philosophy must ask if the object of faith is possible.

* * *

What kind of possibility might characterize faith? Would it be a logical possibility? This would be the case if philosophy could find no internal contradiction, or any reason to affirm or deny the content of this faith. The object of faith would then be, for reason, a freely constructed belief, but one with no connection with the totality of our experience.

What is more, faith would embrace unbeknown to itself the paralogism of the ontological argument, for it would consist in passing from a possible concept to a real existence.

Substituting mathematical probability for logical possibility might authorize calculating the chance of passing from its idea to being, but this would still disguise the ontological argument: and the sophistry would be just as evident: "A mere concept has neither few nor many chances of becoming a real object; it is neither close to nor distant from the threshold of existence. It belongs to another order and has no necessary relation to existence.... From the fact that we are no more authorized to deny the existence of a thing than to affirm it, we must not conclude, as Pascal seems to have done, that there is one chance in two in favor of the existence of the thing."[8]

Consequently, "the sophistry is clear: if the hope of future happiness is based solely on a logical possibility, then we must discard Pascal's wager."[9]

How can the object of a wager depend on a real possibility? On only one condition: if our state in a future life should be a particular case of a kind of existence that already exists here and now, or, what comes down to the same thing, if the present specification of this kind of existence is open to a further specification.

This possibility would be *real* through the general form it has in common with our earthly existence—but it would be merely *possible* if we have no idea of this further specification of the general form given to us here below.

More precisely, it is formal reason, the freedom that constitutes the soul of every judgment and of the will that is the form of our present existence in common with our future existence. But this reason or freedom is only a form, one which calls for some matter. Faith places its hope in a new matter, one adequate to reason, but of which we have no idea here below.

Thus faith has as its object not a state radically foreign to our present life, which would be only logically possible, but an existence or reason that would give itself another matter, another content. This is the real possibility of the object of faith: the substitution of a pure nature for human nature within the bounds of reason.

Philosophy can prepare the way for this hope and even authorize this anticipation by faith to the extent that it can demonstrate the independence of reason from its natural contents, and above everything else the disproportion between form and content.

Reason's independence regarding its present contents is what all of Lachelier's earlier work bears witness to: in isolating the pure consciousness of the ego, reflection has provided an answer in advance regarding this condition. On the contrary, the idea of a radical disproportion between nature and spirit is something relatively new in Lachelier's philosophy. The philosopher of *Psychology and Metaphysics* was more worried about connecting nature and spirit, to finding in nature a symbol of pure spirit: it would seem therefore that Lachelier progressively renounced the symbolism of nature and over time gave greater emphasis to the abyss separating them. The energetic language of *Notes on Pascal's Wager* is truly new: "there is not merely a lack of harmony but even disaccord and almost contradiction between the form and matter of each of our intellectual acts."[10]

Lachelier seems to have taken the opposite road to the one Kant took: in Kant's last work, this was meant to show the homogeneity of understanding and sensibility, the harmony of freedom and nature, which he had systematically opposed to each other in his earlier work. Lachelier, on the contrary, more and more emphasizes a radical disproportion between our intellectual being and our sensible nature, and a total impotence of freedom to create our life, to determine our undertakings overall.

Let us consider the speculative life: reason claims to put the seal of objectivity on the smallest instances of our knowledge; it is an impoverished matter, the point of view of individual sensibility that nourishes such an ambition. The impersonality of knowledge would like to cut its ties to such individuality.

How equally filled with bitter reflections will be the analysis of the will: "In principle we always will that which in itself and in relation to pure reason is best; but in fact we always will whatever our inclinations and our imagination acting together present to us as the best even though this should sometimes in reality be the worst."[11] Will someone say that this must be an accidental aberration of our spirit, a simple error in judgment? No: it really has to do with a congenital powerlessness; we can only necessarily follow the ends relative to our inclinations, our imagination. To take on life, freedom is condemned to deny itself, to obscure itself by borrowing from the fallacious powers of nature. In the human condition, "we can do nothing, we do not even create our own life. It seems, remarkably, that we ought to be able to fully convert ourselves, to divest ourselves of our faults, from one instant to the next, that to do this we only have to will it, and yet nothing like this happens, even when we sincerely will it, which seems to indicate that we only will the idea, and, consequently, that we only have the shadow of freedom within us" (letter to Rauh, 1891).

Undoubtedly it is in this sense that he confronts Kantian optimism with Pascalian pessimism in another letter to Rauh; Lachelier seems to ask himself whether he is for the former or the latter: "Is there in Kant any trace of that anxiety, that feeling of powerlessness which is Pascal's ground? Does he not think, on the contrary, that it is up to each of us to realize the moral ideal, at least through making infinite progress toward it?" (letter to Rauh, 1892).

Yet was it not the same Kantian optimism he professed, a few years earlier, in *Psychology and Metaphysics*? "For we create every instant of our life by a single, self-same act which at one and the same time is present to each and superior to all. . . . In a word, we achieve a destiny which we choose, or rather never cease from choosing."[12]

But this optimism already calls for its counterpart: "Why is our choice not the better? Why do we freely prefer evil to good? Apparently, we must abandon the effort to understand this. Besides, to explain is to excuse—and metaphysics ought not explain that which does away with morality."[13] For to explain something is to demonstrate that it must be; but evil is precisely what is but must not be. Consequently, there is something in nature that spirit does not symbolize, which resists it. For instance, Lachelier writes in 1913, to Gabriel Séailles: "in moral philosophy, I do not think I have anything more to say than what I taught at the École; I ended up with a renewed dualist Stoic conception." As in Stoicism, we are condemned, since in the end it is necessary to act, in terms of certain "preferable ends" which undoubtedly do not have an absolute value; he writes to Émile Thouverez, in 1906, that if duty is absolute, no practical precept is. A large margin does remain for individual initiative. These practical precepts come down to making morality something empirical: it is a question of providing the least disproportionate matter to the form of freedom.

It is odd to see Lachelier seeking the contents of morality in vegetal nature; it is necessary to look there if the higher forms of nature and of living organisms incarnate a bad will; it is necessary to get beyond the complications life brings. It is well known that Lachelier distrusted the will and life. It is what he retained from Schopenhauer's philosophy. He saw how "this world is a test for a will that is indifferent when it comes to good and bad, yet more bad than good, since it is essentially egotistic in each of its concentrations. . . . The true problem of pessimism is knowing whether the 'will' is not everywhere and in every case in humanity a bad power, which it is up to us to liberate ourselves from: this is what, I think, Schopenhauer rightly and profoundly saw."[14]

So we are led to look to nature beyond the will: whereas animality is a second-hand nature, a principle that puts a stop to things and is egoistic, vegetal nature is unaware of egoism and individuality; on the contrary it is a principle of indefinite expansion: "Not that egoism and struggle do not lie within the heart of vegetal life, but their existence consists in constantly going beyond themselves, in incessantly producing new existences; each one, in being good for itself, is therefore good for others, absolutely good" (letter to Séailles, August 14, 1883).

Here is the secret, not only of an empirical morality, but of an empirical politics; vegetation teaches us an anti-democratic lesson: "It is the latter nature that, through its expansion, creates families and states, and, depending on the time and place, diverse organisms, but following a law of hierarchy and subordination" (ibid.). "Nature," he also writes to Victor Basch, "nature in vegetation and the lower animal societies has outlined in advance the plan of human society. The leaf is not a flower, the worker not the winged ant, and there are, in an ant hill, more workers than winged ants, and in a plant, when it is grown, more leaves than flowers."[15]

It looks as though Lachelier found himself more and more pessimistic: and this is the profound meaning of his anti-republicanism. Victor Basch has correctly stated: "I am well aware that socialism is very optimistic, that it has faith in the perfectibility of the human species. But, at bottom, every social doctrine that wants to live and be realized must be optimistic. Socialist optimism consists in taking every man as capable of feeling the higher joys, that everyone can become aristocrats, following an appropriate education, and to differing degrees."[16]

In Lachelier's correspondence we find a growing doubt about the collective salvation of humanity. The more he saw what was happening around him, the more he had the growing impression that humanity was heading for a fall and darkness.

* * *

The abyss, which here below separates freedom and reason on the one hand, and sensible nature on the other, attests to the possibility of a rupture between our reason and our nature: "Thus reason and liberty clearly overflow our actual consciousness. In us they are the partly indeterminate idea, the half-empty framework of a spiritual life quite imperfectly realized in this world, but which may be much better realized in another one if all the sensible elements of consciousness were removed and the matter of intellectual acts were to become proportioned to their form."[17]

But this real possibility of there being an object of faith does not lessen the real merits of this faith: "There is in this, however no proof of the reality of a ultraterrestrial future."[18] And Lachelier is happy to discomfort reason regarding its highest hopes. Who knows? This opposition of reason to its content can only be a stimulant: "In the presence of a non-arbitrary ideal which answers to a subjective need of our reason but whose objective value, nevertheless, reason is powerless to establish, what can one do except to believe, to hope, or, as Pascal suggests, to bet?"[19] "If the syllogism fails us here, then let faith take the risk, let the wager take the place of the ontological argument."[20]

Is this to confess powerlessness, failure? Not at all! But both philosophical honesty and a feeling for faith's autonomy. Lachelier holds equally to the fundamental distinction between reason and faith and also to the necessity of their union. There no longer is any passing from reason to faith other than the causality of finality. From the formal to the living God, there is no analytic development, the latter being indemonstrable and transcendent. Lachelier always set aside all intermediary knowledge that was not that of pure reason or pure hope: "Religion is the orientation of the whole of life toward the beyond; asceticism and mysticism are vigorous but bold efforts to force the barrier at the present moment."[21] For the same reason, he protests against Blondel's philosophy, which would like to lead us progressively to a doctrine of transcendence through a method of immanence. There is no doctrine of transcendence. The letter he writes to Blondel, in 1896, is quite telling: "Is it not to play with words to say that the very idea of immanence calls for that of transcendence? . . . I would say that through reason we reach the word, but only within ourselves, as a formal principle, and exclusively as rational, and that it was necessary that it teach us through a fact that it was at the same time love, in order to reveal to us a full reality and a principle of life, what until then was only a form, a law, by revealing itself as transcendent in that it is one with the Father and the Spirit."

This is why he says to Boutroux: "Our certainty about the beyond will begin with the experience of the beyond. Let us be content, therefore, with expectation, with believing, with a rational, reasonable faith, something that is not yet given us to know. A simple faith which affirms the reality of the beyond with its eyes closed is better than an alleged science which, in passing too easily from the idea to being, risks grasping only an ideal being."[22]

But just as important, this concern to safeguard faith is meant not so much to preserve the believer's merit and faith's dignity as to safeguard God's domain, the space of grace and the initiative behind revelation: this is what stands out in the lines he wrote to Blondel and also in the older letter to Ravaisson in which he speaks of that "idea of an absolute in general which we would be powerless to determine or which we might have room to believe really undetermined and chimeric, if revelation properly speaking had not come to teach us that the substance of this absolute is love [*charité*]" (letter to Ravaisson, May 4, 1871).

So must we consider faith as a purely speculative hope? In a still older letter to Ravaisson, he said: "As soon as an ideal appears to us as possible, we are absolutely obliged to want it to be a reality and to act on this supposition; it is in this decision of the will that moral faith consists for me, which is not the *fides ex auditu* [the faith that comes through hearing], but which may, in turn, serve as its base" (letter to Ravaisson, August 8, 1868).

But how are we to act, how are we to knead nature to make it symbolize the divine nature? In truth, it seems that, for Lachelier, the notion of a symbol should have yielded its place to that of sacrifice, renouncement, emancipation: Schopenhauer is someone who invites us to liberate our will precisely in this way.

Would it be an exaggeration to say that the idea of liberation, of emancipation, in its plainest sense, should be the general, speculative attitude a thinker should practice faced with a finite world? In his essay on "Sacrifice," Lachelier writes: "Even today, in the ideal of monastic life, in the sacrificing of nature, there is something that surpasses morality, which even contradicts it in the sense that we ordinarily understand it. . . . The basis for all this seems to be that the finite does not subsist apart from the infinite except provisionally and thanks to a tolerance regarding which we may well believe we should renounce."[23]

Reabsorption of the finite into the infinite seen from here below seems a vain idea. It is only in the beyond that the real is reconciled with God as fulfilled. Here below emancipation is the rule governing our attitude regarding the world.

B. What Idealism Accomplishes

Philosophy demonstrates the possibility of faith. May we not say, without going beyond our texts, that it calls for faith in order to get beyond an ultimate impasse? Pure reflection stops at a vanquished idealism; through faith, we complete idealism: for, in God alone—the God of faith—nature is posited through reason.

Lachelier's philosophy has too often been considered complete; it is the man, not the philosopher, who prolongs it practically through faith. It might be better to say that without faith philosophy is an incomplete cycle, and that faith is an indispensable link for thought.

But it is necessary to step back a bit. We know that Lachelier believed it was necessary to surpass Kant in the direction of an absolute idealism: "Reason is the thing-in-itself," he writes to Rauh in 1893; "Kant's only mistake was to leave subsisting, beyond reason, the possibility of a thing in itself." So absolute idealism was forced to provide a proof that Kant did not provide. If reason is the thing-in-itself, it will not be truly absolute unless everything is internal to it, unless we can rest with an idealist monism, where reason is not just a form, but is creative of its matter, where sensibility reenters the rhythm of pure thought, where the fact is reabsorbed into the right, the given into its value. Critical idealism was content to lead to the given in terms of its formal conditions; one could not require it to state the reason for the agreement between the form and the matter of knowledge. Absolute idealism promises something more. If reason is absolute, it must not only be self-sufficient; it must explain everything. Lachelier was well aware of this: "The legitimate development, the only legitimate one, of Kant's philosophy consists in saying that what is at issue here is not human thought, but absolute thought, and that the idea of being creates being, including what, in being, appears least real and most foreign to being" (letter to Janet, 1891).

We know what *Psychology and Metaphysics* was meant to achieve: symbolism would take the place of the reduction of nature to an ideal, as much from a speculative as from a practical point of view. But beyond the arbitrary character of symbolism, we can ask whether Lachelier did not subsequently give this up. With the *Notes on Pascal's Wager*, a gap opens between nature and freedom, between sensibility and reason. Leaving aesthetic symbolism on the practical plane and returning to Stoicism's dualism leads to an identical opposition on the theoretical plane.

In our human situation, we are capable of only a vanquished idealism. In a letter to Jean Jaurès, already cited, he shares his doubts: it is perhaps an insolvable problem for idealism "to demonstrate how being, in all its degrees and forms, proceeds from the different forms of the idea of being . . ." It seems we are driven back to two hypotheses: either a radical dualism, from antiquity or Manicheanism, or a degradation of being. "Perhaps it is necessary to frankly admit outside of being a principle of its unfolding and for the sensible manifestation of this idea, Aristotle's ὕλη or at least Plato's χωρά; in any case this must not be the first idea, the still abstract and empty idea, which, through its futility, would make spirit vanish, turning it into matter, and thought into sensibility" (letter to Jean Jaurès, 1892).

Finally, the philosophical perspective that imposes itself is that of the superimposition of two worlds: the one described by Hume, the other by Hegel: "I would say that for the idealist there only exist representations, sensible, individual ones and intellectual, impersonal ones."[24]

Therefore it seems impossible to maintain both the ideal of the absolute purity of spirit and the interiority of the world to spirit. This is also the conclusion of Brunschvicg's philosophy.

* * *

So faith, in surmounting the dualism of reason and matter, completes idealism: "There is at least one thing we can admit without completely understanding it, the existence of a thought that would have no need, as our does, of an empirical content, but which would give itself to itself or rather which would be for itself a content of another order and consequently would alone be what ours cannot be in its union with nature: a complete, real, living being."[25]

Would absolute idealism then be the object of faith? Things seem to lead to this. Lachelier writes in his text on "Réalisme," "everything which is an object of thought is different from the act of thought[,] and thought cannot draw its object out of itself. But this is owing to the fact that thought is not what it desires and ought to be, i.e., intuitive. For if it were to be intuitive, its object would not be external, but immanent—or rather the two together would be only one and the same idea or truth."[26]

Intuition therefore is the point where religious hope and philosophy's ideal converge. In God alone, reason's ideal is satisfied.

But it is true that idealism is fulfilled only as hope, that faith does not abolish nature, it only prophesizes its disappearance. Idealism is fulfilled only in a state of transcendence, in a beyond; it is in this same sense that Le Roy writes: "God is what idealism lacks."[27]

Our idealism therefore remains a vanquished idealism inasmuch as we are merely human. The human condition condemns us to always live short of our better self, to leave our nature on the margin of reason's ideal and faith's anticipations, merely hoping for a unitive life with the living God.

Now, why does idealism find fulfillment only ideally? Why does the reduction of nature to freedom not happen here below? Why is our idealism here and now vanquished? Why does the imperfect remain short of the perfect, we might even ask ourselves, why are we not God?

To answer this, we would have to show how the imperfect proceeds from the perfect without diminishing it, how this genesis of nature is not a degradation of the absolute, but in some sense an enrichment.

Still, I ask myself whether the traditional problem of nature's creation belongs to philosophy or if it is not, in the end, God's prerogative, impenetrable to human points of view: "The ways of God are not our ways," says the Old Testament. Maybe man's road leads from the world to God, but the movement of God toward the world is precisely what is incomprehensible to us about God. This opposition in two directions between what Plotinus called procession and conversion is perhaps one of the fundamental forms of the distinction between mankind and God. God has no need to reconquer himself or to become more in order to be; but, on the other hand, he is the one who creates what is finite. For man alone, spirit needs to rediscover itself; an ascending dialectic is properly a human dialectic, but it can no more engender nature than install itself in being apart from a prior conversion. The divine point of view would be procession, the human one conversion. This may explain the certain failure of every genesis of the finite.

It is true that Brunschvicg criticizes a basic equivocation in the notion of creation. For him, conversion is the only real creation, for it really is a progress toward illumination; creation that would go from the absolute to the relative would be a diminution, a degradation; but perhaps it would be better to say that from God's point of view, the position of the finite is really an enrichment and that creation in the traditional sense of the word is, in its own way, progress.

Bergson writes: "As a matter of fact, the mystics unanimously bear witness that God needs us, just as we need God. Why should He need us unless it be to love us? And it is to this very conclusion that the philosopher who holds to the mystical experience must come. Creation will appear to him as God undertaking to create creature, that He may have, besides himself, beings worthy of His love."[28]

But to correctly understand these lines, it is necessary to understand mysticism, Love, and the notion of the Person, all of which have no place in an intellectualist philosophy and an impersonal idealism.

PART II

Lagneau

Introduction

Regarding reflexive method, Lagneau says: "This method is both experimental in its starting point, which is observation, and rational by nature."[1]

To find thinking, therefore, is to start "not from the abstract in order to construct the concrete," but from the highest, the totally concrete, in order to decompose it into its elements (Spinoza's Metaphysical Method). But where do we find this integral psychic and metaphysical fact? Not through deduction (which would be a vicious circle)—deductive method is not a means of research—but through analysis, starting from some partial fact, or partial facts, by taking them apart and discovering what they lack, what they presuppose. "But this is not by a deductive method."[2]

We start therefore from the most unpolished given, the most rudimentary manifestations of thought: from perception; we look for what makes perception thought; is it through what, in it, is pure sensations and what is simple, sensible presentation, or is it through the implicit use of a higher faculty?

By a kind of anatomy, we are going to "analyze" this apparently unified complex of perception, to decompose it into an intelligible form, which is the very nature of our understanding, and into sensible matter. Then, reflecting on this intelligible nature caught up in perception, we will ask ourselves on what conditions we can make legitimate use of it. We shall discover that the least thought brings into play, beyond the understanding, affirmation and the use of a judgment of an absolute value, which is the very being of thinking, absolute thinking, which is in agreement with its works.

Lagneau sums up this regressive analysis as follows, but in a reverse order: "Let there be a thought, it *produces*"; "Let there be its form; it simply *is*"; "Let there be spontaneous awareness beyond any form; it *is not*"; "One observes only its *becoming*, that is, the matter in the form, in order to disengage the former from the latter."³

This reflexive movement is largely Lachelier's, but Lagneau prefers the negative method of the night of understanding to the positive method of intellectual intuition. The higher degrees are attained only in what the immediately prior degrees *lack*. One grasps in what sense Doubt takes the place of Intuition, and in what sense a radical absence will provisionally take the place of a direct possession of a total Presence.

I. Awakening Thought

Lagneau establishes that a spontaneous understanding, an operative and direct thought, are involved in perception in the most precise and most complete of his *Essais*: the *Cours sur la Perception*.

The exergue could have been this assertion from his *Fragments* cited earlier: "spontaneous awareness, apart from any form, does not exist."

His analysis of perception illustrates the general idea that the lower presupposes the higher and that a partial element of knowledge is explained only by the Whole of Thinking.

It would be the most serious illusion—the empiricist illusion—to believe that perception is a passive imprint: it is an act of spirit; active verbs express it: to perceive is to *connect* sensible qualities to places and objects, to *determine* the nature of an object, its dimensions, on the basis of intuitive indicators.

But it would also be an error to believe that it is the most rudimentary elements that support the most evolved ones; for instance, it seems that we interpret the nature, size, and distance of an object on the basis of what is intuitively perceived. The order of dependence is just the opposite. I judge the sensible properties of objects only through the idea I give myself of orientation, of distance, etc.; if I look at a landscape painting upside down, the colors appear strange and new. This is close to a raw intuition detached from any interpretation, but it is not really a perception.

Will someone say that this orientation, this distance, is a raw given? This is not so. I represent distance to myself only on the basis of the idea I have of magnitude; for here, too, I interpret the raw intuition as a function of an idea. That man, whom I see over there, and standing in that square, I grant him a man's height only because I know it is a man, and this is an idea, an act of understanding. Thus I first assume that this patch has to, with the scheme for a man, this hypothesis, which is a conception, allow me to grant him a true size; then, in comparing the true size, which is conceived with the apparent size, I evaluate the distance, and this distance allows me to *conceive* the true colors despite the apparent colors resulting from the lighting and orientation.

This analysis of a partial fact reveals to us the general nature of thoughts: "the lower functions of thinking are only conceivable through the higher ones; the lower beings, those which make no use of the higher functions of the intelligence cannot perfectly accomplish even the lower functions. . . . The lower carries the higher; but this is only the order of facts; everywhere in thinking, it is the higher that explains the lower."[1]

We could come back to this theme is many ways; it is a point on which converge multiple partial analyses: let it suffice for us to mention two original analyses, that of the sense of effort and that of listening to music, which are profound, and in any case newer than the classical analyses of sense illusions, double perception, the third dimension, etc.

It would be a contradiction to say, following Maine de Biran, that one feels being active: feeling is passive. Yes, there is some passivity, something purely given in the feeling of effort, but what is given is precisely not the effort but the modifications of our organism. The active element comes from elsewhere: it has to be revealed to us somehow; without it we would not distinguish an automatic modification from a voluntary one. The active element is the idea of a movement that is to be produced: "We do not feel ourselves to be active, we judge ourselves to be so."[2] The feeling of effort is situated at the junction of the intellectual element, which is the part that is our activity, and the physical remainder, which is purely felt: "To feel oneself active, is not just to experience a sensation, it is to affirm the connection of a sensation with an idea under which an effect was pursued."[3] This is a situation that has no equivalent that offers reflection an occasion for endless deepening. Our Whole is engaged in this feeling of effort: if we consider that that effort indicates the connection of a sensation with an idea, it must be said that it implicitly encloses a causal relation between our thought and sensible nature. Moreover: the judgment of causality is not yet experienced as an undiscussable necessity. "Necessity cannot be felt; it is affirmed as having to be. Which is why this action itself cannot be explained apart from the affirmation of a freedom that submits to necessity only because it judges and evaluates it."[4] Hence the theory of judgement and the Problem of God are immanent to a problem of perception.

Now consider another partial fact: listening to music. In the sound, there are two things: a pure quality that is sensed, a tone, loudness—on the other hand, an element of measurement, of quantity: rhythm. "Through hearing, we determine the parts of time, just as through touching we determine the parts of space."[5] The first group of elements—tone, loudness—is purely felt, but it is not experienced unless it is inserted in a quantitative order—that is, an order of implicit evaluations, of spontaneous judgments.

So in hearing music we find our mental life figured, just as in the relation of thought to nature: "In thinking, there is room to consider two terms: nature with its indefinite movement which escapes determination; and about this nature, and constituting its truth, there are determined thoughts. Thinking thinks everything as measured; thinking is measuring."[6] In the same way, like a symbolic game, "two elements are perpetually found in music: one which is abstract, the music; the other which is concrete which is the melody; the melody must bend to the authority of the beat; it is this battle which gives rise to musical emotion in us."[7] Music is therefore an occasion for us to see and to find, for "our inner life cannot be sufficient by itself; it must seek its being outside itself and ground itself on the universe before reflecting on its own existence and representing it to itself."[8] Was it not Lachelier who said in the same sense that thinking can find itself only in things, and to find itself it must first lose itself? It is therefore also true to say that the smallest spectacle of our nature is an occasion for philosophizing, and that philosophy can be born only in contact with present life.

If therefore "the determination of meaningful knowing goes from inside to outside, from the higher to the lower," we can talk about a raw sensation only after the fact: it must have been determined by our mind, must have been developed as perception, and must have been conceptually fulfilled for us to be able to descend to the raw impression: "We *conceive* perception as having a first impression, sensation, as its condition; but we discover this state through the analysis of perception as complete; it is a condition that we separate, an abstraction. We cannot experience its pure state; so we speak of it negatively as a 'change produced in us not dependent on us,' as something 'independent of the reaction through which thought masters it,' pure passivity, multiplicity, diversity."[9] We do not know pure sensation, therefore, except as a necessity for explaining thoughts. We have just one way to know this for ourselves: reflection. Does reflection then make us conscious of anything other than spirit itself?

We must therefore say: "It is by something other than sensation that we come to know sensation, for it does not reflect upon itself."[10] Through a new effort of reflection we must now attempt to awaken this implicit understanding, become conscious of it, make it the very object of reflection.

* * *

It is necessary to renounce finding the Whole of Thought in sensation. Sensation is not self-affirming, it is thought only because it is included in a higher thought: "To represent something to oneself is to affirm the being of these representations, and consequently under a more or less vague form, to conceive them: it is through the idea that any representation gets determined."[11]

Will the picture of spirit be completed if we simply add the intelligible form, our understanding, to sensible matter? Is the life of the mind limited to applying an intellectual nature to a sensible one, to determining the undetermined sensation through a system of categories? That in brief is pretty much the ideal forged by Kant: "the understanding is intellect insofar as it seeks to connect its representations to itself, to its own nature."[12] But this is nothing more than an act of science: to apply the understanding to sense data is to determine the laws of nature: the understanding therefore reduces to the faculty of experience. We know that Kant acknowledged no other legitimate use for thought than this work of understanding. The imperfection of thought for him was not that a gap always remains between this ideal of rationalization and the obscurities of sensory matter, which cannot be reduced into intelligible relationships. Perfect thought would be the limit toward which thinking aspires when "it *tends* to represent the world to us as an abstract mechanism to which every sensible phenomenon is attached."[13]

Must we then believe that thinking is absorbed entirely in seeking the laws of nature, and that "reality is only this conception of experimental science"?[14] Knowledge—does it come down to linking a sensible *nature* to an intelligible *nature*?

Not really. A whole cycle of problems is opened, given our uncertainty. I am not a machine that applies methods, rules, ready-made laws to a sensible universe. That is not thinking. Thinking is not a mechanical understanding. Thinking goes beyond the problems raised by such use of the understanding, to that obscure zone to which we apply such vague terms as: ground of the understanding, value of the understanding. Thinking cannot be saturated by reducing matter to the form of cognition. It goes beyond this to ask by what right this intelligible nature has precedence over sensible nature, to ask whether we do not falsify things when we make them pass through spirit's twists and turns, concerning which we do not know why things are this way rather than another. Discovery of the understanding, which lies dormant in perception, must be followed by a second awakening: beyond understanding there is thinking, which questions itself about its destiny and poses at least two questions, even if it is not prepared to answer them: 1. By what right does a form apply to a nature that is foreign to it and undertake to absorb it? 2. What is the value, in itself, of this understanding? To pose these questions is to refuse to take spirit as a fatality, as a ready-made nature, whose reason we do not grasp. Thinking is what, in us, judges understanding.

It is necessary therefore to pass to a second degree of reflection: what am I, I who think the world? Am I doing things in the right way by being scientific? Here, in truth, there is really only one problem, for the value of understanding is precisely the value of reducing sensible nature to intellectual nature. Understanding the nature of things and understanding the nature of thinking are one and the same thing, for, if the laws of spirit are arbitrary, they disguise things, and a vast veil of suspicion is thereby cast over the world. So, it is one and the same thing to ask under what conditions the forms of the understanding are no longer simply imposed and under what conditions I make proper use of them in applying them. If I find no absolute ground for the forms of knowledge, the very consistency of the world disappears. We shall rediscover the solidity of the object only when every suspicion of arbitrariness when it comes to the nature of thought will have been set aside. So there is just one problem: to seek what things are and what makes thought valid. At this second degree of reflection, the lower is still explained by the higher.

Now let us transpose this epistemological language into metaphysical language. It is this transposition that we find in passing from the *Leçons sur le Jugement* to the opening pages of *De l'existence de Dieu*. We will encounter, in fact, no new idea. But we will situate things from the perspective of the problem of God.

To say that "the life of the understanding does not suffice by itself"[15] is to say that the system of laws and things cannot posit itself as absolute. If we call necessity this level of thought, where the contingency of sensible nature is absorbed into the necessity of intellectual nature, it would be necessary to say that God is not this necessity. Nor is it in relation to Kant that we are situating ourselves here, or even Spinoza, who has given us the type of a philosophy of necessity. We must renounce the illusion of a mind closed in on itself and confined to science, of a God entirely absorbed in the necessity that underlies this kind of knowledge. God is what posits, not what is posited. God is the ground of our understanding.

It is not helpful if we correct the insufficiency of understanding by associating it with sensibility, for the reciprocal dependence of necessity and contingency indicates their respective infirmities. The lower presupposes the higher, but the higher needs the lower. If things draw their consistency from the thought that lies dormant in them, this thought is condemned to be a thought ballasted by matter. An incurable insufficiency weighs down the work of knowing due to the fact that it has two roots. The purity of spirit is in itself sterile; it becomes fecund only by participating in the insufficiency of the sensible. The absolute, therefore, cannot be by necessity conjoined with contingency.

In any case, if the absolute were to lie in the commerce of the understanding and sensibility, the fundamental problem would always remain. Understanding does what it must do in interpreting sensible nature in terms of its own nature: "However necessary a truth may be that is proposed or imposed on thinking, from the moment it affirms this thought to be true, thinking separates itself from this thought, it considers itself consequently as not being entirely absorbed by this truth, as not having a nature identical with it, or to put it better, it considers itself as being something more than everything that has a nature."[16]

So a second mirage dissolves: just as a pure sensation is a contradiction in terms, an absolute necessity is a purely ghostlike image. An absolute necessity may not be affirmed. God therefore can be pure necessity only on the condition of our not knowing that. To think necessity is to add something to necessity. To be distinct from necessity, to be opposed to necessity. The vocation of reflection is to awaken this ground of thinking that gets uncovered lying behind the least judgment that something is true; every thought presupposes an implicit act of faith in the value of thinking: "Objective experience assumes and conceals a metaphysics."[17] To think is implicitly to grant an absolute value to knowing.

"Thus the absolute reality we seek, the only one that fits God, is neither existence nor being, for with existence and with being, what really is, is not contingency but value."[18] "God would exist only through an absolute act of freedom through which he proclaims his reality. Being can never be grasped from the outside, experienced [*subi*] by following the path of meaningfulness, or by that of intuition. If something is, this is because thinking would have it so. But why does it want that? The source of all being must lie in that act by which thinking establishes that there must be something there."[19]

Pure freedom therefore is the ground of thinking. It is necessary to see clearly what, above all else, Lagneau is trying to hunt down: the most insidious form of realism, the realism of thought; realism is not given; for if absolute thinking came about through a simple assertion that something is evident, this would always be only a fact, and we would have escaped the mirage of the thought-object only to fall back into that of the thought-thing: "Thinking presupposes an action, is an action, and the idea of action is not exhausted by the idea of necessity."[20]

Lagneau knew Spinoza all too well not to be struck by the mechanical character of understanding. As Alain puts it: "Our demonstrations and calculations imitate the things that unfold in them rather well."[21] Indeed, was it not Spinoza himself who pictured the understanding as a spiritual automaton? Spinoza's illusion is more profound than Kant's, for it is more conscious of itself: "Spinozism is a kind of *a priori* empiricism: it is the negation of spirit and of every power higher than facts; we can say that Spinoza reached only what, in us, thinks without us. This is not really us, this spiritual machine that only redoubles the first machine. Thinking is an action: for it, to be is to create, not to be submitted to being."

* * *

Let us look back over what has been said: sensation *assumes* the understanding; the understanding *assumes* the value that is pure action, pure freedom. Will this reflective movement therefore be a deduction, a demonstration? Starting from the presupposition that something is, we asked under what conditions there can be something. Each new degree of thought is posited as the sole justification of the lower degree. The higher *explains* the lower. Thus, what *must* be said is: "[W]e can indeed experience things, we know whether they are, if we do not go so far as necessity."[22] "In the same way, for necessity, we *must* affirm that the act through which we grasp it in things is what must be and the fact that we experience this is the result of an absolute act through which thinking posited this necessity that we now experience. For a mind that refuses to admit the value of thinking, of its necessary forms, nothing really exists."

This reflective movement mimics a demonstration by absurdity. It is contradictory to deny God, for "this world considered apart from the absolute act of the mind is nothing, can only be affirmed through a sophism, a contradiction."[23] But if so, we arrive at this singular contradiction, which is that it is necessary to affirm freedom. The mere stating of this warns us that we must be dealing here with a simulacrum of a demonstration. The order of demonstration is precisely that of necessity; the passage from necessity to freedom cannot be of the same order as that of a demonstration. This is a surprising conclusion, which for all that is not meant to place its dialectic outside logic. Above the plane of logic extends that of deciding, of the pure affirmation of freedom. Lagneau therefore links up perfectly with

Lachelier: dialectic is an absolute movement of discontinuity, in which necessity is necessarily affirmed and freedom is a pure act of freedom. Philosophy lies in the pure movement through which we become free, for freedom is nothing outside of this movement of freedom.

Hence, God, conceived as the free affirmation of value, is sovereignly indemonstrable—owing not to a weakness of our understanding but to a radical incommensurability between freedom and any proof. One does not demonstrate God; or rather, because these terms leave room to believe that God is distinct from the act of thinking that reaches him, it is necessary to say that God, pure thought, is not of the order of sensibility nor of that of understanding, but on the plane of a pure positing that affirms itself through itself: "The source of insight [*intelligence*] cannot be in the understanding, which recognizes necessity, but in the power of affirming what must be."[24]

What still needs to be explained is the simulacrum of the demonstration of freedom: this illusion stems from there being a human point of view, which is not God's point of view. Explanation, for man, consists in starting from the conditioned in order to arrive at the condition. We determine the starting point in terms of the point of arrival. But this is to invert the true order of dependencies. Starting from the world in order to arrive at God, we pin God to the world. We could call this illusion the retrospective illusion:

> The necessity to affirm this reality relates only to a particular individual assumed to exist. It appears only when one considers a given existence. . . . The appearance of the anteriority of the law leading to action exists only after the action has been constituted. It is because we are constituted in this way that we cannot not be dependent on the absolute, that we cannot avoid seeing the freedom in our acts as depending on a law that is prior to our freedom. But this is not the point of view of what is absolute. In the order of the absolute, freedom does not depend on the law, just the contrary.[25]

In reality, a thing is given only through the affirmation of a value implicit in it. A being knows its own existence only because it has implicitly first posited the value of the Whole of Thought in affirming its own existence. So reflection does not consist in deducing freedom from necessity, in making freedom arise from what it is not, by deducing God from a world that is not in any way divine and that is radically bereft of God; it comes down to becoming conscious of what we possess without being aware of it. A broadly universal truth that overflows the framework of Lagneau's philosophy: we do not introduce the absolute into a soul that is bereft of it; which is why we do not demonstrate God. We simply reveal him to souls that unconsciously possess him in what they experience; it is not a question therefore of discovering a radical alterity, a pure transcendence, but of something more intimate to us than ourselves that we incorporate into the least of our certainties. This immanence of God signifies that there are no isolated certainties starting from which we can pass through a logical connection to other self-sufficient certainties; every certainty rests on the unique certainty of God. Passage to this ultimate certainty is not through logic; it is a passage from the implicit to the explicit, an uncovering: "Through reflection we do not reach God outside ourselves as a separate reality from our own reality; in reality, we do not reach God, instead God reaches himself in the very act through which we posit some thought as true."[26]

Undoubtedly, logic does have something to say; undoubtedly, we can remind the man who denies God that his position is not tenable and that he posits his own reality through what he denies, and so, in denying the conclusion, he also denies its starting point. But, in fact, one is never led to God in this manner. It is necessary to take the royal road of a free decision, whereby God reveals himself to be [*se pose*] within us. It is this pre-eminence of a decision over the tortuous path of providing a demonstration through an argument from absurdity that Lagneau expresses as follows: "It is never as a result of the mere impossibility of maintaining both being and the negation of absolute reality that absolute reality is posited in a particular being. . . . It is only when one starts from the fact of the existence of some being, when one considers it as already given, that one can be led to represent to himself the impossibility that, in this being, an absolute affirmation must not also be given for anything to be. . . . On the contrary, it is because in this being the affirmation of what must be is posited that this being knows itself as existing."[27] Which is to say that God is not the endpoint but a starting point. In us, reflection revealing what we do imperfectly invites us to a conversion through which, by renouncing what we take to be our perspectival center, we attempt to assume God's point of view. This is a significant affirmation: through this conversion we are God, because God is not distinct from the act of thought that contains him; he is this very affirmative act.

This God, Lagneau tells us, is Descartes' God, but stripped of the sophistry of the ontological argument; in fact, at the start this act is not foreign to us: but "Descartes refuses to place this absolute freedom of God within us, in every act of thought. . . . He places it in a region that is transcendent in relation to us."[28]

But precisely because he is transcendent, Descartes' free God has to be demonstrated. Contrary to this, for the perspective of immanence, discovering God is a problem of becoming conscious [of God]. It is uniquely a question of consciously repeating the creative Fiat that we carry out unconsciously and of comprehending that this Fiat does not have to do with a distinct object but rather is God himself; second, a more serious reproach, the realism of ideas leads Descartes to deduce God's existence from the idea of God. But if we comprehend that God is not distinct from the act that apprehends him, there is no fatal passage from the idea of God to God. God is the very act we carry out to the extent that we are totally free: "Thus, this analysis through which we have demonstrated the inferior reality that constitutes existence, and the reality that constitutes being, in presupposing something other, the other posited through freedom, leads us not only to the affirmation of God's Existence, but to God himself, and we can only comprehend this, and through it everything else, on the condition that, at each instant, God's act realizes thought in us."[29]

* * *

But, once again, what is this act of God? Is it something of a strictly intellectual order? Is it that intellectual consciousness Lachelier spoke of? Is God a pure idea? Here is where Lagneau and Lachelier differ. For Lagneau, it is true that the least act of thought envelops the affirmation of the absolute—on the other hand, there is no act of thought that expresses this adequately. Purely intellectual reflection shows itself to be impotent when it comes to apprehending God. It can reveal God only through the very infirmity of the act of showing, of affirmation, of proof. God can be given to us only through the doubt that reflection brings to bear on the sufficiency of necessity. God is in what the proof of pure thought lacks, the very fact that "thought never finds complete satisfaction in the mere intuition of necessity."[30] The demonstration of the Existence of God lies in "the very impossibility of Thought ever demonstrating its value to itself."[31]

Lagneau therefore will embrace the negative way, that of radical doubt, at the very moment where Lachelier tries to realize a positive genesis of thought through a synthetic method. Alain reports this remark by Lagneau: "Oh! Behind Monsieur Lachelier is the Gospel."[32] He insinuates that this penetrating conception of doubt could not appear in Lachelier's philosophy. It had to have been something conventional, playful—a theoretical embarrassment for a thinker who pretends to look for his path but never strays: "It is impossible to believe that Catholic doctrine, so explicitly metaphysical and even didactic, does not provide this thinker security regarding what is judged, or, if you will, thought, fully thought, to which spirit must finally and always conform itself. . . . A Catholic does not bear the burden of thinking everything. Someone does it for him. He is saved in this way from the absolute despair that Lagneau at least once referred to."[33]

But an adequate understanding (*intelligence*) of what doubt is, is still required. Doubt introduces us to truth because doubting is not the pure absence of thought, its total abstention, but a premonition of the more and more pure conditions of truth, which are satisfied by no affirmation.

Absolute doubt is not an absolute refusal to affirm the anticipated possession of an absolute demand for truth: "When one doubts, one knows however that there are absolute reasons to affirm or deny something."[34] Doubting tells us that mind has become more or less obscurely conscious of what a pure truth would be. If thinking doubts the value of its nature, it is because it does not see evident reasons in this nature for affirming its value. To accept this nature, to accept it without discussion, not to doubt it, is to be blind regarding what thinking lacks: understanding gets walled in, does not raise itself up to God: "Doubt is a certain awareness of ignorance."[35]

With doubt the true nature of judgment becomes apparent: there is more in any judgment than simply an apperception; the idea is not simply given and experienced; it is approved: "The given—the related-idea—is dominated by something of a different order."[36] This action, which adds itself to a thought, comprehends it, surpasses it, approves it, appears in an irrefutable way in doubt. Thinking's act of positing something appears there in a negative form. The possibility of "positing" a thought appears in that of "deposing" it. If nothing exists except through the "yes" of thinking it, its "no" is the clearest verification of this; the power to agree is experienced through that of being able to refuse to do so.

It appears, therefore, that doubt is the sole introduction to the plane of freedom. We do not escape legality, necessity other than by posing a question. No question without some uneasiness, without pausing our spontaneity: "It is really in the act of doubting that the creative action of thought is found. So long as thinking applies its forms, without doubting whether they fit the objects to which they are applied, it does not really know anything. Doubt therefore is a realization of thought."[37] A "critique" of the act of judging therefore is, in the complete and current meaning of this word, a judgment and a doubt: "Critique, philosophical reflection that comprehends our nature and frees us from it."[38] Not comprehending is not experiencing the truth. "Like something given that would be external and to which we would have to entrust ourselves."[39] Not comprehending is being duped when it comes to certainty, being credulous. Comprehending is being incredulous.

Does this mean, for Lagneau, that doubt should be enjoyed? No: to doubt is to suffer; it is an ascetic introduction to true certainty. It is much closer to the negative way of mystics, to the dark night of understanding, according to Saint John of the Cross, than to Montaigne's "what do I know?" Doubt which constitutes our human dignity breaks with the innocence of an earthly paradise, with childish serenity; with reflection, suffering enters the world.[40] Through reflection, an abyss, a breech gets opened between the thought fact and its legality, its approbation. The value judgment by which man grants confidence to all his affirmations in the age of innocence was wholly entangled with the matters known: "The man who has never reflected does not doubt for an instant that he sees reality as it is. . . . The child only sees what is: everything for him is unified and plain."[41] But when thought awakens, it feels stretched between its body and its soul: "the primitive unity finds itself broken by the opposition between the determined external knowledge, phenomenal knowing, justified by experience and internal knowing, by right, that results from spirit's pure action."[42] The dawning of reflection "is the dawning of suffering, that is, of feeling the gap between the real and the ideal, the given and the possible."[43] Lagneau more than anyone has emphasized the dissolving character of reflection. Reflection "analyzes" thought—no longer in the sense that it moves back from some resolved problem to its conditions, but in the sense that it decomposes the lived unity of thought, like anatomy, or rather a vivisection.

* * *

But Lagneau is not a dilettante. Doubt is a necessary phase, but a dangerous zone to cross. Indeed, we may find an identical accent in other thinkers who are not suspected of dilettantism.[44]

Doubting for Platonism is a conversion. The captives in the cave are minds who experience what is true without comprehending it. Doubting is the liberator that unbinds the captive and allows him to turn toward the sun and freedom. But the free man will not be able to enjoy this expected freedom, which does nothing and creates nothing. The captive returns to the captives: doubting is not an end in itself; the free man will take up the charge to think and to will, but this time he will no longer be bound by the chains of truth; he will accept them: "Reflection must lead us to that state where the mind no longer sees the truth as foreign to itself, where it sees it as its own work, perfectly understood and rendered in some way completely transparent."[45]

Dilettantism and skepticism are not supportable positions: "simply being acquainted with things, toying with the opposition between one's reason and nature means floating indefinitely in the void, taking reason as something external, which one makes use of as viewing, *ut remfruendam oculis*, enjoying the show, amusing oneself using one's reason. One can go on forever using this kind of freedom, this state of suspending things, examining things, doubting, being independent; dilettantism, irony, skepticism."[46] What our dilettante has not taken into account is that he has dug his own grave. All reality vanishes for him, as he does himself, along with the world, he with his precious egoism. The world we must not forget is not something self-sufficient that we simply experience. The world has a meaning only for spirit. It is thought that realizes the world. If thought no longer has a meaning, neither does the world. An abyss opens between appearance and being. The world becomes an illusory reflection of our accidental constitution: "The sensible world, the object of knowledge, no longer has a meaning, no longer having an absolute meaning."[47] Hence an alternative imposes itself: either thought is valid, and the world takes on consistency—or our intellectual structure is not the expression of the absolute, and the world it has elaborated sinks into nothingness. Do we give an absolute meaning to thought and to the world? "To answer no is to make the world and oneself unintelligible, to decree chaos, first of all in oneself. But chaos is not nothing. Being or not being, selfhood along with everything that is, one must choose."[48]

But are we capable of remaking what reflection has unmade? Are we capable of surpassing the sterile freedom that opposes itself to being and existence? Are we capable of the act "that at every instant realizes the world for us, realizing it in the sense that, at every instant, the reality of the world is what we will it to be, that is, the result of the value we attribute to thought within ourselves, that is, absolute thought"?[49]

II. The Conditions of Certainty
The Monism of Thought

Reflection has led us to a kind of dead end: the necessity on the one hand of affirming God at the cost of not being able to think, the impossibility on the other hand of demonstrating God. From this there is a paralysis internal to thought, a radical doubt.

On what condition can we leave doubt behind? If we cannot straightaway install ourselves in a lived certainty, at least we can have a sense of its border; under what conditions do we rediscover, having reflected, the certainty that thought has an absolute value? We experienced this certainty without knowing it, prior to reflection, in thought's age of innocence, in the least of our intellectual acts. But reflection has occurred; and the act of knowing has become paradoxical and impossible. Sensible nature and the understanding have shown themselves to be incompatible. What is more, the very nature of the understanding has become a scandal for thought.

In innocent thought we enclose in one and the same act perception, understanding, and thought's approbation of itself. Thought's innocence is its unity. The solution, then, is that we must rediscover this intellectual unity within reflection—that is, first of all sensible nature and intellectual nature should be fundamentally one and the same thing, and their distinction an appearance, a lack of comprehension; second, this unity must not be that of something whose nature is ready-made in us at every instant. The identity of the existence of being and of value—the identity of contingency, of necessity, and of freedom—this is thought's ideal: "We can seek to determine the truth of things only if, preceding this, God places within us, through an absolute act, something valid, and real owing simply to the fact of this validity. This act is the act through which God constitutes himself."[1] And a bit further on: "God is the identity of the real and the ideal; to put it a better way, the identity of matter and the pure act, of its form and this action."[2]

* * *

But we need to be careful that we are not just playing with words. This solution is not simply ready to hand; stated this way, it is just a bunch of words. What a failure it would be for reflection, if having accepted the burden of radical doubt, we could get out of it by a simple verbal assertion. What needs to be signaled here is the tragic contradiction in this solution: on the one hand, we cannot fail to get out, but on the other, this is totally incomprehensible. It is not by waving a magic wand that we get to the necessity of freedom and the sensory appearance of intelligible truth. Lagneau, with his continual distrust of easy solutions, is there to remind us to be modest. We do not really understand these words, or rather we do understand that the solution lies here, but we do not really comprehend what an underlying unity of the real and the ideal signifies. We do comprehend that it is necessary to posit God, and that God is the unity of every degree of thought, yet we do not comprehend the unfathomable richness of this solution. It is impossible to get beyond this double demand. To ask, "What am I?" yet hide behind a lazy diagnostic would be to forbid the very possibility of thinking and doubting. To remain asleep, on the other hand, on the soft bed of easy certainties, by offering definitive explanations, which fill the spirit, by embracing a glimmering deism, would be to accept magic solutions. What glows is rarely true. This is the deep insight of Lagneau's philosophy. No, we can be neither agnostic nor deistic. Therefore it is really a question of constantly opposing the necessity of a solution and its incomprehensibility.

* * *

Lagneau outlined the solution to the problem in the opening pages of his *Cours sur le jugement*:

> For purely representative life, unity . . . ; for the life of understanding, duality appears: spirit is conscious of itself and knows that it is distinct from the objects it is aware of. . . . But it is impossible that thought should rest in any other way than on the insight [*intelligence*]

into the identity of these two terms. So long as thought does not comprehend how its own nature is at bottom the same as the nature it grasps in the object, it is faced with a mystery. It remains caught up in doubt, in uncertainty. . . . For rational life, our mind comprehends the relation of identity that exists between itself and the thing to which it applies itself.[3]

The natural tendency for the understanding is to absorb the real into the intelligible, to dissolve the opacity of the concrete into the limpidity of the abstract. This effort is valuable only on one condition: that, in absorbing the real into the intelligible, we get to the deep meaning of the real. This demand of reason necessarily arises at the end of the Kantian critique. Lachelier encountered it. He also recognized, in the purely Kantian position, an instability; he wrote: "The legitimate development and the sole legitimate one of Kant's philosophy consists in saying that it is a question here, not of human thought, but of absolute thought, and that the idea of being creates being overall, including what, in being, appears to be least real and most foreign to being" (letter to Janet, 1891).

For Lagneau too, the condition of certainty is the fundamental identity of the intelligible and the sensible. Reducing the real to the intelligible must not falsify it but instead grasp its true reality. This is what must be understood: the identity of the particular and the universal:

> To say that a proposition like "snow is white" is true is to say that it is true for every mind, that is, that it expresses, in a particular form, their unity. But this unity breaks into two parts: their intellectual unity and their sensible unity; the proposition has to express both things, that is, it must express that the sensibility that experiences the whiteness of snow relates to every actually given sensibility just as my understanding relates to all understanding. Furthermore, this proposition would not be true unless it simply signified that my understanding and every understanding must apperceive as necessary the relations among the different elements that make up the sensible matter of the proposition; in this case, the necessity will be applied externally to the matter, that is, the proposition will not be merely subjectively true. If we assume that universal understanding is not at bottom the same as universal sensibility, no truth. Whoever says something is true says not only that we perceive this necessarily through our own laws, even if everyone agrees; if someone says we see things as they are, it is necessary to say there is agreement between sensibility and understanding not through an application but through a participation in one and the same principle.[4]

This passage is particularly obscure: but we can't blame Lagneau for this, because here is precisely the supreme enigma, the mystery that explains everything. We can, at least, elucidate its terms; through my sensible constitution I am bound to an individual point of view: no one else sees exactly the same snow, for my situation *hic et nunc* is unique. But through my intellectual constitution I coincide with every spirit; in truth, there is just one spirit. This, then, is the problem: a proposition stems from applying a universal intellectual form to an individual sensible matter. The proposition will be absolutely true on only one condition: that my individual point of view not be a relative one but that "the sensibility that experiences the whiteness of snow relates to every actually given sensibility." The core of the mystery is the idea of a universal sensibility. A few of Lagneau's assertions seem to indicate a step in the direction of the sensible: "To affirm that something must be is to affirm that there is a truth about what is, and that what must be is compounded with what is." But other assertions seem to indicate that it comes down to sacrificing the sensible and the individual, "everything real in the individuality about which we say something is what is universal." Philosophy's final word, the ideal of reason, is therefore to say that the intelligible is the true nature of sensible, the universal, the ground of what is concrete; we see what obscure grounds of being these assertions introduce: it is necessary to comprehend the eternal meaning of the present moment, the total presence in the actual and particular, the subsistence of appearances. Lavelle's philosophy makes similar claims. For him and for Lagneau it comes down to something more energetic directed against phenomena:

> In affirming that we are, we affirm that being is. The result is that the center of the world, in us, is shifted, that we recognize that our reality consists in what, in it, is posited by the total being on which our reality depends. To grasp what we really are for this hypothesis would be to grasp at a given moment our relation to the absolute whole, which would be to resolve our individual existence into universal existence. We can only truly be if, as individuals, we are only pure appearances, while our true reality consists in what there is universal about us, and which we find in everyone else.[5]

This ideal solution points us down the path of the highest idealist ambitions: toward nothing less than the idealistic search for the unity of subject and object, of intuitive reason beyond what the understanding provides.[6]

This is what would be necessary to comprehend in order to give completeness and validity to the least of our thoughts; but this is what we do not comprehend. It is true to say that the deep-lying unity of matter and form alone can give validity to thought; but it is also true to say that the understanding can conceive of matter and form only as radically distinct. Is it not in the discordance between them that Lagneau discovers the secret behind errors and doubt? Error occurs when the relation proposed for our affirmation which is forged within us, independently of us, as a result of habit, of an automatic mental mechanism, leaves out a confrontation with the rules for truth, which are distinct from the simple apperception of this relationship. This relation, which is proposed but does not get judged, affirms its right to truth. To make a mistake is to omit evaluating, judging the perceived relations, to be "fooled by habit, to experience a representation as it is brought about by the ordinary movement of everyday thought, by the mind's automatism, by nature."[7]

The analysis of errors therefore attests to the radical distinction of levels of thought.

What is more, it is this most shocking disproportion, the most self-evident scandal, the inadequacy of our sensible nature to our intellectual nature: every truth appears as incarnate. The general nature of a triangle can appear only clothed as some particular triangle. Therefore I am pulled between two natures. As a sensible being, I am bolted to a point of view in space and time, to a perspective that strictly characterizes my individuality. I am the only one to see this triangle from this precise aspect and at this precise instant. Two men never see exactly the same thing. Sensible representations oppose men to each other. We do not see what a universal sense experience would be. But as spirit, I am capable of discerning the universal nature of the triangle and of coinciding with it along with every other mind. The idea unites, it is one, there is an impersonal spirit present in everyone. But this is the scandal: I raise myself to what unites only through what divides. It is useless to minimize the role of perception, to make it an occasion, a shock that awakens the purity of the idea and posits its autonomy. Kant has cured us of this Platonic or Cartesian hyper-spiritualism and reminded us that intellectual knowledge begins from our senses. Lagneau is particularly faithful to this point of view: "If we conceive there is truth, we do so as the truth of what we experience sensuously. The order of intelligence rests on that of sensibility."[8] It is impossible therefore to abolish one of the two terms. How, then, are we going to be able to talk about their identity? Was it not their evident disproportion that awakened doubt in us and introduced us to freedom? It seems as though all the earlier analyses testify against there being a final solution. There is no peace possible between being and existing: "Never, properly speaking, in any of our knowledge can we find the justification for the affirmation we make of its truth; never, in other words, is the matter of the truth adequate to its form."[9]

The day when this disproportion burst into our mind, we suspended our judgment; we doubted and became free. Are we going to relinquish that freedom? Lagneau testifies against himself: "A mind that becomes conscious of the disagreement that always exists between what it affirms and what truly is can no longer get rid of a kind of philosophical doubt. We are free so long as we always hold on to a mental reservation."[10]

* * *

So we find ourselves torn between two demands: to give birth to freedom by recognizing the distinction and disproportion between sensibility and our understanding. To give birth to certainty by positing their identity. Should we not say that the point of view of this distinction is apparent and symbolic? But before considering this solution, we need to consider a second aspect of the problem.

* * *

We have really looked at only one face, or rather one degree, of the problem: not only is it necessary to comprehend that the nature of things and of our mind are one and the same nature, but also it is necessary to postulate, without being able to embrace its full meaning, the fundamental thought that this double nature is at bottom freedom, a decision, a choice, a fundamental Fiat.

Our regressive analysis has led us to place freedom above necessity: to comprehend necessity is to free oneself from it.

A provisional attitude, an essential liberation, an inevitable moment for reflection. But a moment for crossing through, for surpassing: this freedom of expectation must become a creative freedom. Gide's way of thinking—before it came along—never seduced Lagneau: not to commit to something in order to be free to commit to anything, to hold oneself in reserve through an egoistic enjoyment of autonomy is not a tenable position.

It is necessary to think, to act, to commit oneself.

But how, then, can thinking not be a return to slavery, to the discipline of being rule-governed? On one condition, that we comprehend that discipline and rules are the ground of our freedom—but that this affirmation will take on its full meaning only on the ground of practice. We state it here in its theoretical purity before any clarification that comes from action. A freedom that creates a law—or, better, a law that is basically free—is what must be understood if we are to exhaust the plentitude of the least act of thought. Thought is truth and because of this, necessary; what must be understood is that this is not something experienced, not an ultimate given, but what founds, what gives.

The vision of our dependence on everything is overwhelming and crushing. The words *submission, dependence, resolution* in the All[11] seem to negate spontaneity completely. But it is precisely the opposite that needs to be understood, that this dependence of a part on the Whole is access to the freedom of the Whole.

> The affirmation that the true reality of every being is universal is nothing other than what constitutes the pure act of freedom. . . . To act freely is not to act apart from every necessity, which would be a pure nothingness, but to posit necessity itself as an expression of absolute, that is, of universal reality. . . . Freedom does not directly conceptualize itself, the absolute for which freedom is one aspect is only conceivable as an action through which a particular nature, experiencing in itself the universal being on which it depends, affirms the reality of this being in willing that it should be.[12]

Lagneau shows the depth at which metaphysics is completed, the horizon on which every aspect of thought converges: it is necessary to grasp the core of two philosophies for which we catch sight only of their disjunctive truth: a philosophy of Being which would at the same time be a philosophy of Freedom. It is necessary to conjoin the evasive unity of these two words: Act and Being.

But we do not really understand this unity: we can only be subject to its truth and accept it. We do not really see what a truth would be that would be free without being arbitrary. We do not really see what the unity of the act of thought which is free and the object which is its outcome would be. At best, we can conceive of a freedom that accepts the truth, adheres to what is intelligible, bows to the necessity of reason, but a freedom that posits thought as a whole? . . .

It would be faithful to Lagneau's spirit—for whom the final solutions lie on another plane than that of the understanding—to affirm the profound obscurity of this solution. Thought can occur only through the necessary duality of two aspects: thought is the experienced object and is the act of thought. All the *cogitata* impose their necessity, and it is the *cogito* which is a free act; in other words, a judgment and a concept, the thinking subject and the thought object. But I do not believe that this amounts to the opposition between what is thought and what is unthought, but rather, as Maurice Blondel puts it, it is the opposition between thinking and what is thought, a drama internal to thought: the *cogitata* are thoughts, the *cogito* is the thinking of them.

Does Lagneau believe in an easy, intelligible reduction of the act of thinking and the thought-object to one and the same thing? It does not seem so. His whole analysis of judgment, which depends on the understanding, testifies against such an assertion: judging presupposes an apperception, a given; this apperception is undoubtedly the result of older judgments, but this infinite regression does not allow us to envision a final absorption of the concept into the judgment, of the thought-object into the thinking subject, of necessity and freedom, Being and Act. The duality of the relation to an object and a judgment is insurmountable. A judgment is essentially adhering to a content that presents itself to this judgment. But we can only adhere to this content, not draw it from ourselves. Absolute idealism has always tried to absorb the object into the act. For it, everything is judgment. It takes a stand, therefore, against thought as a type of realism, as itself a thing, which would subordinate the judgment to its concept.

Therefore it is once again necessary to place the unity of thought, which gives it its truth, which imposes itself on spirit, on the plane of what is incomprehensible. We do not know what an act-truth is, what a subject-truth is, a truth that does not impose itself but that is the work of thought. This duality of the two aspects of thought shows through our language. To think is an active verb—that is, an act turned toward something, an act that expects a complement. Knowing implies an intentionality, the expectation of an object, as the German school of phenomenology has demonstrated.

Therefore this second aspect of the solution has led us to an antithesis: thinking is free, for were it to be determined, there would be neither truth nor error; it would simply be what it has to be. But truth remains an act of submission.

Therefore we are still divided between two requirements: on the one hand, having to posit the identity of freedom and the law; on the other, not being able to make sense of them as distinct. Does this mean that the divisive, divided point of view of our intelligence is the final word when it comes to thought, and even a complete illusion? This is what now needs to be considered.

* * *

Unity can be the ground of reality only if we grant an illusion inherent to our understanding as a counterpart to it. This powerlessness of the understanding along with its counterpart, the necessity to go further and posit God on another plane, we already saw at the end of the preceding chapter. But, in truth, it is not a question of the *insufficiency* of reasoning or of any proof: what must now be denounced is a certain *falsifying* of what is true, inherent to our understanding. The point of view of the absolute is the unity of the planes of thought. The point of view of our understanding is their distinction. The whole prior analysis turns on this idea. Reason postulates the unity of three planes of thought (the free positing of value, the necessity of truth, and the contingency of sensibility), but the understanding can conceive of them only as distinct. Of these two theses, the one is true, the other apparent. Unity is the point of view of the absolute; diversity is man's relative point of view.

Understanding "explains" this unity. We have to take this term in its most radical sense: understanding "develops" the unity of being:[13] "In the absolute, nature, truth, and the ideal are one, and it is on this condition of the underlying unity of these three necessarily distinct terms in the eyes of the understanding that the reality of nature and the possibility of science and of a moral life can be conceived."[14]

Therefore we are obliged to grant that thought, as unity, is refracted on a relative, apparent plane, which falsifies to some extent the plane of unity. The absolute "manifests" itself (φαινειν = phenomenon, appearance) in a trinity. These three terms "are not separate from one another other than in virtue of a necessity, in other words, through an act that does not grasp reality as it is but that disperses it in order to explain it."[15]

Afterward, the understanding corrects this distinction through a correlation which is a relating. Through this relating the understanding stitches back together what it had previously cut apart. Relating is the remedy for its infirmity: relating substitutes solidarity and a logical connection for the true unity: relating is the human symbol of unity.

A very deficient substitution, for through our intelligence it restores the supra-intellectual unity of three planes of thought. It connects them through two contrary reasons, both of which are illusory. We know the first of these. The pseudo-deduction of truth, starting from contingency, of freedom starting from necessity. Here is the second one: if we envisage freedom, we are forced to incarnate it in a law: "It is through the very fact that we begin by conceiving freedom, the pure action that we conceive to be real, *therefore* as already having the form of a law, a truth. But now where does this law come from, unless there is not already a nature within it? For whoever talks about a law says that something is bound, whoever talks about form talks about the matter to which this form applies."[16]

We see the illusion in this double connectedness: we have conceptualized the relation of the understanding to the infra-intellectual and freedom in terms of the understanding, that is, of conditions: "Whence it follows that freedom itself, under the form we have conceived of this absolute, appears to us again as necessarily having its conditions in other terms."[17]

It comes down, therefore, to transcending the understanding and, with it, the order of explanation, and of passing to life as a unity, which implies not only a break with the illusion of sensation, with the illusion of the sufficiency of an idea, but also with the illusion that sums all this up: the appearance of the diversity of aspects of being and of thought.

Philosophy consists in this ultimate effort, and it is in this highest sense that it consists in passing from appearance to being. To pass from appearance to being is to pass from a chopped-up symbolic vision to a unitive vision.

This idea of a symbolic value to the understanding allows us to make more precise the problem of *participation*. Lagneau writes: "If one says that one sees things as they are, it is necessary to grant an agreement between sensibility and the understanding, not through an application, but through participation based on the same principle."[18] To say that the many participates in the One does not mean that the many comes from the One through a generation of physical types or through a deduction of logical types, but that the many is the human symbol of unity. When Lagneau says that it is necessary to conceive unity not "prior to one or the other term, but above both of them," he wants to state the exact character of this participation. It is not first of all God who next engenders freedom, truth, and nature, but, in the absolute order, there is God, and below on a human plane, which symbolizes the preceding one, the trinity of Being. This "below" does not express a preeminence of the true over appearance. "The absolute cannot be found other than above every explanation, what is explained and its explanation—that is, in their unity. Above the act of understanding, whose object is to determine necessary relations, there is a place for the act of pure thought, which consists in affirming the identity of those terms that the understanding, subsequently, will develop."[19]

But, truly speaking, to pass from the conception of the diversity of orders of thought to the comprehension of their unity, to pass from appearance to being, is to pass from the intelligible to the incomprehensible: "The highest act of thought consists, definitively, in comprehending the necessity of positing the incomprehensible."[20]

Scandal, will cry the Priests of Clarity: we believe we know what a sensation, an idea, above all an idea, are; we even have clear and distinct ideas of them, like the triangle and infinity; you have come to upset our intellectual security, you have told us that we do not really understand what a pure idea is; and you explain things by what is incomprehensible.

Lagneau has, effectively, denounced the root of atheism, the idolatry of clear ideas; a complete knowledge, closed in on itself like Parmenides's sphere, knowledge without any fissure, has no need for any other foundation. God is above all what our knowledge and our action lack. Blondel, in his recent book, has denounced the latent atheism of Cartesianism, found in every religion of clear ideas, all forms of positivism: we do not have clear ideas, we do not have certainty that is sufficient by itself alone. This is why there is no paradox in saying, with Lagneau, that metaphysics consists in explaining *obsurum per obsurius*. Jacques Rivière writes, in his book *À la trace de Dieu*, these lines which will no doubt throw light on Lagneau's profound thought:

> To be aware of the reasonable character of mysteries means dealing with souls, that is, with getting used to explaining some things by other just as obscure things. In psychology, the obscure is clarified only by what is more obscure. To know more about something is to discover what is more and more strange. Each new clarity about it leads to a new contradiction discernible in it: we understand what happens better, because we distinguish in it something yet more incomprehensible. When we come across an unforeseen action of a being we thought we understood well, we always see afterward that this was owing to our not having seen it as complex, as inexplicable as it is in reality. As *inexplicable*, that is, as impossible to fully unpack: as impossible to arrange all the elements of its character side by side, without its squealing due to this arrangement.[21]

But can we, through an act higher than understanding, penetrate this incomprehensibility; is not this incomprehensibility external to us: in us is something external to our understanding. Therefore it will require an *action of the absolute* to engender certainty about the validity of thought. What is more, this action of the absolute cannot be realized outside of nature as a whole. This act of the absolute must, in being realized, make us comprehend the identity of the ideal and the real, the unity of being and the degrees of being.

Therefore we must pass from a reflexive and purely speculative attitude—that of a spectacle—to a prospective and active attitude, the regressive analysis has to turn into a conversion, and our questioning freedom, which is the freedom of reflection and doubt, must turn into creative freedom. Here is where practical reason, action will introduce us to the solution we were looking in vain for on purely speculative grounds. The final word of reflection is its application in favor of action: "So long as one proposes to demonstrate the validity of one's own thought, one poses a contradictory problem: begin by constituting the unity within yourself and reason will be justified; otherwise, it is absurd to want to prove that God is. The act of moral freedom is the only possible solution to the problem that arises regarding the validity of thought. Everything will become clear for a consciousness that began by wanting the good."[22]

It now will be a question of following Lagneau on this road, where action is going to save us from the deceptions about what is incomprehensible: "Philosophy is reflection that ends by recognizing its insufficiency, and the necessity for an absolute action that starts from within."[23]

"Philosophy is the search for reality starting from reflection, and next leading to its realization."[24]

* * *

But before following Lagneau down this road, it will be good to draw together a few reflections on the deep meaning of this monism. This monism is more audacious than that of Lachelier, who is content to attach nature to the ideal through symbolism and does not go as far as asserting their identity. Toward the end of his life, Lachelier even renounced absorbing the real into the ideal, at least from a strictly philosophical perspective. For Lagneau, on the contrary, the real is strictly identical to the ideal, but at the same time, there is at least one thing that remains outside the absolute: our understanding. The problem remains therefore of the genesis of illusion and of the appearance inherent to our understanding, the problem of the relative is merely shifted. Why is our point of view not that of God? Why is what appears to us not what it is? We are obliged to systematically oppose our understanding of God's understanding: "This is why Spinoza said that if we attribute understanding to God, it is necessary immediately to add that there is no more resemblance between divine and human understanding, as we understand it, any more than between the dog constellation and a barking dog."[25]

Lachelier would never have written these lines: precisely because Lagneau's monism is more complete than his, a greater margin remains between human nature and the absolute. For Lachelier, sensible nature, matter as understood by the understanding, is irreducible to the absolute, but through its form this understanding, our understanding is rigorously identical with divine understanding. Lagneau distinguishes himself therefore from Lachelier when he asserts that human understanding is misleading, that its divisive, analytic illusion cuts it off from God.

Another opposition results from this: because human and divine understanding are irreducible to each other to Lagneau's eyes, speculative philosophy ends up at the incomprehensible and we must say: "God is essentially incomprehensible, and every expression that tries to convey him can only be an identification of what he is, in essence, just the opposite, irreducible."[26] On the contrary, because human understanding is not mistaken, but incomplete in Lachelier's eyes, a positive intellectual intuition is possible, and we can directly grasp God's act within ourselves, God as formal. Faith does not go beyond this act; it fulfills it. Here is the deep reason for the difference in accent between these two great philosophies: Lagneau prefers the negative method to that of the positive method of an intellectual intuition, because he finds darkness and illusion there where Lachelier believes there is light.

If we may call transcendence this irreducibility of God to the understanding, we can say that it is necessary to grant an even greater transcendence between man and God when we push the monism of thought even further.

Lagneau never says the word *transcendence*, but the idea is implied by his whole critique of our understanding. No doubt we need to be clear regarding this transcendence. God is transcendent only in relation to one aspect of our thought; a radical transcendence regarding the Whole of our thought would be totally incomprehensible: God is not outside us; in us, he is what goes beyond understanding. A margin of transcendence therefore does not suppress immanence; it corrects it.

I believe that other considerations could add to the necessity for this corrective, including those having to do with the notion of the person: for Lagneau as for Lachelier, the impersonality of thought is closely tied to the thesis about the unity of thought. And yet, no one more than Lagneau has insisted on the responsibility of thought and its needing to doubt: doubting, questioning, wanting, being free and being responsible, are these not strictly personal acts? Lagneau does not seem to think so. For him there is no middle term between the limited horizon of our individuality and the impersonality of thought: "Our true reality does not lie in our particular reality, but in what, within it, is universal. . . . To grasp what we truly are would be to grasp at a given moment our relationship to the absolute whole, it would be to resolve our individual existence into universal existence. . . . Our true reality lies in the universal in us which is found in everyone."[27]

I believe consideration of the unity of being must be simply completed and corrected by our consideration of concentrating on being in free and responsible personal locations, but not bound to it. Otherwise, all the meaning of any basis for an inquiry into being would be lost.

Furthermore, for a philosophy that affirms what being must be, evil must be unexplainable, for evil is what ought not to be; perhaps only a certain autonomy of the person can explain evil. It is true that our true being is "our relationship to the absolute whole" and that "what in us is universal and found in everyone."[28] But this reciprocal interiority of persons may not be incompatible with a certain distinction.

But Lagneau allows only that a diversity of being or of beings must be due to a lack of comprehension.

How does Lagneau, therefore, intend to safeguard the unity of being, which is that of thought, despite the evident disproportion between divine and human understanding? It looks as though, toward the end of his book on the existence of God, a middle term does intervene between unitive reason and analytic understanding. Lagneau has seen that the thesis of the unity of the forms and functions of thought would mean the abolition of cognition: "intellection assumes that at bottom it should be true that the universal is the reality of the particular; but the particular cannot be purely and simply resolved into the universal, for then there would not be anything."[29]

Therefore if a total absorption of the particular into the universal entails the abolition of cognition, their unity must not be conceived of as a fact but as a limit, a tendency.

It is this notion of a limit or tendency that serves to mediate between the two rival assertions of the necessary unity of being and the no less necessary distinction between the real and the intelligible: "A rational act would be to discover the unity of nature, that is, of reality in itself outside the self, after having looked for it, that is, by means of a second act. This rational act must not be conceived of as a movement, a progression, through which the reality of nature would be grasped; this act is never completely realized, it is just the absolute affirmation implicitly contained in every relative affirmation."[30]

Hence the thesis of the unity of being and the identity of the particular and the universal takes on a more subtle meaning. The particular would not be identical with the universal, but a *tendency* toward the universal. This notion of a tendency will find its full meaning only on the ground of action, but it already has a meaning in Lagneau's eyes on the purely intellectual plane, although this remains extremely obscure: it comes down to "an inner solicitation, through the presence of the form of the universal in the particular," or to "the internal action that develops the thought of the idea of universal being."[31]

The obscurity of these lines stems from their being only a trace of the notion of a tendency and of a desire from the plane of action on that of cognition.

The true ground of nature therefore is not static, and the true explanation is not mechanism. Nature is not being as given, but being in the process of giving itself. Existence is becoming, a trending. The true explanation is one in terms of finality. The omnipresence of the whole in each particular being is the presence of a goal, which is that of the universal.

But what, then, is the vision of a universe that *tends* toward the unity that is absolutely true? Or is it still that of a substitute for complete unity, the result of a dispersion through the prism of the understanding? Are the universe and thought—which are the same thing—a unity or the aspiration for unity? It is impossible, in the final analysis, to decide this equivocation. Yet it does not seem as though the thesis of unity is finally abolished. In these same pages, Lagneau writes: "to know is to implicitly affirm the absolute identity of what one knows and the form of necessity that one applies in knowing it."[32] It is reasonable therefore to conclude that the tendency toward unity, the aspiration for unity, is still really only a substitute for true reality, a lack of comprehension.

Therefore the whole problem still remains, human understanding remains external to absolute thought, like the final appearance that falls short of being [*en déhors de l'être*].

The moment has come to pass from reflection to action and to look for unitive thought on this plane.

III. Certainty and Action

It might seem extraordinary, and even paradoxical, at first sight, to make the theoretical problem depend on the practical problem, reflection on action. An old opposition separates science and conscience. Kant is responsible for this. What, above all else, it is important to do is to show that moral conscience is competent when it comes to science, that practical reason and pure reason are not distinct but fundamentally one: "There are not two reasons in us, not one way for seeking what things are and another for seeking what we ought to be."[1]

This important text will be the center of our first comments. How radical the opposition between two reasons was for Kant is well known; no doubt they shared the formal character of unifying every mind, of being the function of universality. But at least two characteristics oppose them to each other: pure reason is relative, whereas practical reason is objective and absolute. In fact, form applies only to the appearances of things. The things in themselves—God, the world, the soul—we do not know what they are, at best we know that they are; they constitute something unknowable which one cannot further or contest.

Practical reason, on the contrary, through its postulates entails an objective affirmation of God and the soul.

A second characteristic opposes them: theoretical reason, which is relative alone, is certain and indisputable; moral faith is only hypothetical.

We already know that Lagneau was against the so-called self-evident and indisputable character of theoretical reason: "Kant grants that there is an experienced certainty which is that of knowledge based on experience and that it is sufficient on its own terms."[2] In other words, he poses no problem about the value of forms of knowledge, as though the nature of mind could be taken for granted. In Lagneau's language, the forms of mind are experienced, not posited; to posit them it would be necessary first of all to have doubted them.

Things are different with moral faith: we say moral faith, and not practical reason, for duty is just as necessary and indisputable as is our intellectual constitution; but, for Kant, moral faith is distinct from practical reason. The former has to do with duty; the latter is constituted by the set of postulates for practical reason, which are barely distinct from the affirmation of duty; faith in God, therefore, for Kant, is relatively independent of the certainty that goes with duty. This is why it is merely hypothetical. This point is crucial. The discussion of it occupies the first sections on the existence of God: God is implied not by the positing of duty but by a need of our sensible nature: this was Kant's error. It is only because we have a need to believe that our experienced opposition between nature and duty, between happiness and virtue, is not definitive that we posit God. God, for Kant, is the rational principle that must be postulated to realize the unity to which our nature aspires. This natural need is undoubtedly rational, because it is subordinate to carrying out our duty, but it is only a need and the postulate of God's existence, which follows from it, participates in its weakness: "It is therefore reasonable to give in to this natural need which is bound to morality within us, a need that leads us to believe in the immortality of the soul and the existence of God. We do not find it impossible to believe this, or even to believe that duty without this belief would be irrational."[3]

Because duty is absolute, the object of faith linked to it is equally absolute, but because the natural need that leads to this faith is hypothetical, the object of faith is equally hypothetical: "If duty is not God himself, it is like the door to the absolute that opens for us."[4] It is this distance between the certainty of duty and faith in God that Lagneau means to fill.

Lagneau has to offer corrections on two points: 1. To demonstrate the close unity between the problem of God and that of duty; 2. To reground the unity of the problem of duty and that of knowledge.

God's immanence to duty is a key idea. Kant was wrong to conceive of God as the absolutely real, the highest thing in itself, as radical transcendence. So put, the problem of God is not solvable, for there is no access to the real other than through intuition, that is, through sensation. Kant never suspected "that God's reality might not consist in existence. He lets us suppose that the ideal of knowledge about God would be to perceive God as existing, for the only things known as existing are those we perceive."[5] Kant's initial mistake therefore was to pursue a contradictory God, a God-object: "Without a doubt he does not look for God in nature; he only looks for reality within us; but he still is looking for a transcendent reality."[6]

In the act of thinking that rises to God is the whole reality of God: God-act, God-thought and not God-object: "It is necessary to see that God is a moment, a natural degree of the action through which thought reaches God in this very thought. . . . the act through which the reality of the absolute is posited."[7] This reversed perspective is nothing other than the passage from a latent realism to a radical idealism, from transcendence to immanence. What is more, it is the sole way of avoiding slipping the bonds between faith in God and the certainty of duty: a loosening to which the development of contemporary moral philosophy bears witness: "To start from a need without demonstrating its necessity makes a contingent-God. . . . Nothing proves that it may be impossible to dominate it, to smother it."[8]

It is directly in the moral act that God must be reached, "not as an external principle having organized nature in view of the agreement between morality and happiness, but as the immanent principle of the good, which we reach in the moral act."[9] So, God is the very movement of thought that passes from value to duty.

We see the deep unity of God and duty in the idealist perspective. Now it is necessary to show the unity of thought in its practical and theoretical forms. In truth, the prior analyses of theoretical reason prepare the way for this concept: Lagneau's whole effort consists in denouncing the illusion of an order of truth imposed by its self-evidence. Behind the least of our so-called evidence, which we believe we simply apprehend and passively receive, is hidden an approbation, an implicit act of faith in the value of thinking.

With this, science and conscience are no longer opposed as the order of indicative judgments and that of evaluative judgments. The smallest indicative judgment is accompanied by an evaluative judgment. Therefore we are not split in two, we always are making evaluations; it is the same thinking that circulates in our every act of thought; there is not a world of things and a world of values, for the world of things depends on that of truths and this latter is upheld by the value of thinking.

The notion of value, which is ethical in origin, is coextensive with the whole field of thought; in return, that of responsibility extends equally to theoretical life as it does to practical life. We are responsible for our thought,[10] for the "conduct" of our thinking as for that of our action, for the "good use"[11] we make of them. The notion of *de jure validity* therefore has the same scale as does that of value.

Hence theoretical thought is the exact replica of practical thought; 1. it contains an act of faith, a hypothetical, indemonstrable certainty; 2. this act of faith consists in granting an absolute value to knowing: "The absolute is in every thought"; God is not cut off from theoretical reason as Kant thought.

Hence the theory of the unity of thinking is complete. We have followed it inside theoretical thought, which now includes practical thought.

But this comparison between two functions of thinking contains one last treasure, which is the very key to the problem of God: practical reason is not just parallel to theoretical reason, it has a preeminent value, it is able to solve the problem of knowledge. The moral act is situated on a higher level of knowledge than that of the understanding. We know that the value of knowledge can be posited only by an "absolute act of a free, rational will."[12] The moral act is situated precisely on this plane of creative freedom, of choice of some decision. It is even the one truly free act within our capability. Truth, we know, is inevitably situated on the plane of necessity, it is simply recognized and undergone; we do not make the Truth, but we can do the Good. In our effort to pass from the contingent to the necessary and from the necessary to the free, we find the moral act of transcending the plane of necessity. Thus the order of a moral decision will surpass and ground that of any proof.

An audacious crowning of a philosophy of doubt that definitively escapes the seductions of dilettantism to blossom into fidelity, devotion, sacrifice, love. We have exchanged the freedom of expectation for a creative freedom. Reflection is a dangerous weapon: for if it frees us from intellectual idolatries, it threatens to leave us only halfway, in a voluptuous skepticism for some, a cruel skepticism for others. Lagneau's work can be a temptation and a danger: it contains, if we decapitate it, every element of a hymn to doubt: "Once reflection has occurred to a mind, phenomenal knowledge, pure knowledge no longer has any solidity, even as relative knowledge. It definitively loses every value for that mind in that reflection does not lead to a moral life. . . . This act of intellectual freedom, of reflection, through which reason breaks out in a particular mind, must if the problem it raises is to be resolved, be followed by another free act, that of a moral freedom."[13]

The whole spirit of Lagneau's philosophy lies in the feeling of thinking's responsibility: certainty does not lie ready-made outside us; it is not something it suffices simply to receive: "It is a chimera to represent certainty to oneself as being able to be passively obtained, by placing oneself simply in the presence of an object. Certainty is the mind's absolute creation. It is spirit, the absolute, God that creates it in us."[14]

The ground of thinking is therefore moral in essence. Skepticism is always theoretically true, because nothing is absolutely demonstrable; but it is a moral fault, cowardice. It is impossible to disprove it through discussion; we can only reveal its moral roots. Undoubtedly it is absurd, because the doubter undermines the basis of his doubting. But we know the inanity and illusion of demonstrations based on absurdity. Only a call for effort will be able to revive the meaning of the Good, which is that of the True, because it is the meaning of the Absolute.

That skepticism should be, at bottom, egoism and cowardly, that the return to certainty is a return to love, this is what now needs to be shown. Skepticism will not find an illusory demonstrations of the absolute value of truth; it simply will understand the moral meaning of the alternative where it digs in its heels and the responsibilities of its abstention.

* * *

Here then is the originality of Lagneau's philosophy. The moral meaning of thinking; for Lachelier, philosophy works in a purely speculative atmosphere; arriving at a formal and abstract conception of God, philosophy has no more to say. Moral life is merely a corollary of speculative life, moral effort is a symbol for the unity apperceived in God by pure reason, or of the love revealed by faith. Lagneau, on the contrary, means to go beyond the insufficiencies of pure reflection through the moral act: "Philosophy is first the search for reality through reflection, and next its realization."[15]

Nothing in Lachelier's philosophy resembles this phase of Lagneau's philosophy.

* * *

To understand the role of the moral act it is first necessary to disengage duty, using an ascending dialectic, from the illusions of visible utility and even necessity. If duty is not a pure creation, how can we introduce the divine Fiat? It would be a serious error to not discern the freedom the moral act includes; it is an illusion to believe that the Good is passively apprehended, that our whole responsibility consists in conforming to it. It is essential to the final solution that we understand that we make the good through our action, that "the ideal is the product of freedom, or rather it is freedom itself."[16] If the good did not totally depend on us, how would we be able to support the whole complex of certainty, our work, and our responsibility?

The ideal is neither some beautiful nature nor a simply conceived law. It is necessary to disengage it from both concrete existence and from a necessary truth.

1. It is not some beautiful nature, for the different degrees of perfection we discern in nature make sense only in relation to the idea of perfection. Therefore we cannot start from the real to arrive at the ideal, by simply comparing natural qualities and passing to their limit. More and less presuppose a maximum.[17] Every concrete ideal is situated in relation to the idea of perfection. This argument recalls the older classic proof according to which the degrees of being presuppose the maximum of being.
2. Now comes the important point: the idea of perfection is not something we are subjected to, it is posited, willed: "The idea of an absolute good, something perfect, is a secondary idea; it has value, reality only in that freedom is linked to it. We endeavor to find what we should do. But what does duty consist of, at bottom? In our positing act there is a duty. The idea of duty is the projection of this act. The idea of the perfect is the abstract form of freedom."[18]

Duty is not imposed on us like a revelation we undergo. The ideal would not be if we did not posit it: "This perfection cannot be perfection prior to the act that recognizes it as such, that is, it is constituted by the very act of freedom."

No doubt many people would recognize that an act of devotion is freely accomplished: "Being worthwhile is being real for freedom."[19] They will grant that we are free either to conform or not conform to the moral law, but not that this freedom consists in positing the moral law. To the extent that the moral act incarnates God, we may say of it: "We must not say that God posits himself, because he must be, because then why must he be? In reality because it is the absolute that posits itself, with the result that there is true being, that is, what must be. What must be is constituted by the act of freedom. Let us compare this idea to what Kant says: The law of freedom is immanent, not transcendent, that is, when we submit to the categorical imperative, we are not submitting to some alien law."[20]

The whole difficulty lies in this passage from obedience to creation, which is nothing other than the reduction of necessity to freedom. I wonder whether this passage happens as easily as Lachelier thinks it does. If we are careful, we will discern an antinomy which had already appeared on the theoretical level: truth was an object that had necessarily to be accepted, and truth was also a free act, otherwise we would not be able to explain errors. Truth was irremediably caught between the *cogito*'s freedom and the necessity of its *cogitata*: it was a free act and a necessary norm. There are always two philosophies of duty: that of the good will and that of the sovereign good. The former makes duty something to be decided; the latter makes it something to be demonstrated. Lagneau strives to absorb the latter into the former by making it a symbol, a projection: "The only idea we can determine of an absolute good is the idea given to us through the analysis of the good will, that is, in the relation it posits between itself and the moral law."[21] For my part, I wonder whether the moral life is not made up of a synthesis, or rather a tension between these two irreducible aspects of the moral life, between the moral norm and the moral decision, between the law and the act. It is perhaps not certain that we can subordinate or even absorb one aspect of the moral life in the other, as Lagneau does; the tension between a normative truth and a true act, between the moral law and a moral act, is perhaps the final motivation of the life of the mind.

Whatever the case may be, for Lagneau duty is not inscribed in a transcendent world to be intuitively apprehended there or logically deduced from it; it is our work, if by this we mean not the evaluation of what is individual about us, but of what is divine. It is our work if we allow what is more inward about us to act, God himself: "The ideal is not an end to be pursued, nor the abstract idea of a law, it is what freedom freely posits absolutely, what freedom adheres to at the same time that it posits it; this is where it gets its value."[22] Someone may ask if the two expressions "adheres and posits" express a shifting between the point of view of morality as a norm and morality as a decision. Perhaps it expresses only the objectivism of this philosophy of freedom. The ideal is freedom's adhering to the extent that it is the absolute speaking here. In one sense, the moral life consists in submitting to the universal, but the universal is what we carry within ourselves. To say "thy will be done" is both to submit and to take responsibility for a movement, to will the divine will.

There is still more: God, we know, is the absolute of value, but he is also the identity of the real and the ideal. The moral act has introduced us to pure freedom; it also makes us understand what makes no sense on the theoretical level, but without which thinking would remain paralyzed: the unity of the absolute and of nature.

In truth, the ideal first presents itself in opposition to nature—an opposition parallel to the antagonism between the universal and the particular. The question therefore is knowing whether the moral life allows overcoming this opposition and, if not, how it is to be understood intellectually, at least as realizing reason's postulated unity.

Considering this is well worth the effort. The failure of Lachelier's monism will perhaps be set aside by the introduction of the moral point of view. We do not say: if the syllogism fails, faith ought to risk it, but that practical reason assumes responsibility. But then, if the moral act succeeds in grounding the monism of Thought, idealism is not fulfilled by the beyond, but by the actual conditions of existence, and we can do without Pascal's wager.

Therefore we must: 1. Understand that the moral act is the realization of the law in nature and points to the deep meaning of nature; 2. that on the other hand we are aware of the distance which for all that still separates us from the divine unity of nature and the absolute.

* * *

That the opposition of the ideal and nature should be the first self-evidence, we have only to reread Kant to convince ourselves; Kant is correct: "The ideal consists in what surpasses the real. To live the higher life, the moral life, is to raise oneself above the determinations of nature."[23] Duty is what ought to be but is not, for value is opposed to existence and being.

In reality a superficial view, for the moral life consists precisely in reabsorbing nature into the ideal: through it, we realize practically the aim of intelligence, the presence of the universal in the particular. Being moral reabsorbs individuality into universality. If "the moral law consists in the subordination of the part to the whole, of what is to what ought to be."[24] Egoism is therefore the exact antithesis of the moral life. The egoist says: there is only me, for me, others are only the projection of my interests and desires. I am the measure of all things. But egoism is the moral root of the empiricist illusion: "What teaches us that there is only the present, the particular? It is sensibility."[25]

This is a capital moment for reflection: for the assertions of egotism and phenomenalism are indissolubly connected. This knot is where the two Reasons are united; by triumphing over one point of view, we conquer the other. Passing from appearance to being first presupposes that we have overcome egoism. A philosophy of being makes our individuality depend on the Whole, to the point of resolving our individual existence into universal existence; it is precisely in the moral act that we negate ourselves as individuality to affirm ourselves as reflecting the universal: "This is what makes us know that we are not pure appearances, that there are other beings than us, and that it is in our relation to them that our true reality consists. But it is freedom that, at each moment, posits in us, through a creative act, those other beings, without which the individual would not be. This dependence only exists because, at each moment, it affirms itself, wants to be in us."[26] Love makes us exit our individuality, and in exiting individuality it makes us understand that the truth about the individual is the universal.

But here it is important to ask an urgent question: does the moral life consist in affirming being or other beings? Here, I believe, is one of the greatest difficulties in Lagneau's philosophy: for Lagneau, love is the true content of the moral act. But does love consist in re-absorbing our individual existence into universal existence, or in coordinating our personal existence with other personal existences? Does Love aim at something abstract, or does it posit others? It is in this sense that there can be an equivocation between being and other beings in the text cited above. For positing being affirms our *subordination* to an impersonal order which is the order of duty and truth; positing other beings affirms our *coordination* in a spiritual society, a personal world. I wonder whether the essential difficulty in Lagneau's system is that it grounds the certainty of impersonal thought on the certainty that others exist. Several texts could be cited in which Lagneau talks about being and then about other beings. Being is impersonal being, Thought; in the plural, it is persons: "It is freedom at each moment that posits in us, through a creative act, those other beings, without which the individual would not be."[27] "The reality of every being, in nature, results from its relation to all the others, that is, as universal."[28] There seems to be a conflict between two points of view, two schemas: an impersonal scheme, where individuality is an illusion, and where the part is defined only through its relations with the Whole; and a personalist scheme, where the discontinuity in being and the autonomy of persons is somehow irreducible. Undoubtedly, the autonomy of persons does not suppress the unity of being in any way or the immanence of the absolute to any of them; but if it suppresses nothing, perhaps it adds something. The pluralism of beings maybe does not contradict the unity of Being but rather corrects and completes it. Lagneau is correct: "Our true reality consists in what is universal within us and can be found in every being."[29] But this identity does not abolish the distinction among persons. A certain alterity is allied with identity. What is more, Love is above all the discovery of the other, and this is where it truly is opposed to egoism. No doubt the discovery of the other leads us to a more intimate discovery of ourselves, but this cannot be furthered by leaving ourselves behind.

By having the value of thought depend on that of Love, Lagneau perhaps does not demonstrate what he meant to demonstrate; the illusion of the diversity of being. This diversity is more necessary for Love than any other form of activity.

Moral life, says Lagneau, lets us escape the mirage of individuality. But does this re-absorption of nature into the ideal appear to us like a sacrificing of nature, a renouncement, a rupture? That is so. But what is truer, or rather on another level of truth, is that in this way we move to a deeper meaning of nature: "Moral life consists in each moment in freeing us from nature, but this end has a value only on one condition: that, in freeing us from this nature, we conform more perfectly with its true law, because at bottom, nature is the product of freedom. This liberation is legitimate only because, in producing itself, it realizes its true nature."[30]

If we comprehend this, we will clearly have satisfied the postulate of the highest philosophy, "that there is an absolute truth of what is, and that it must conform with what is."[31]

It is precisely this conformity of nature and duty that Kant underestimated in his principal work, *The Critique of Practical Reason*, where the assertion of their opposition predominates—yet glimpsed in his subsequent work, *The Critique of Judgment*, where the theme of reconciliation predominates. How would we ever be able to carry out a good action if our nature did not make it possible? More precisely, our nature approves of doing its duty, before and after any moral act. Do we not experience a certain penchant, a natural interest or at least respect for doing our duty? And once this duty is accomplished, does not nature reply secretly with joy, with satisfaction, which is duty's echo within nature?

Let us be clear about this: our reason, our conscience, are not something alien that must be introduced by force into nature which is severed from them. One does not introduce someone by force to a truth he is radically deprived of; otherwise how would he receive it if he did not already have it, deep within himself, as a secret pre-possession? The appearance of rationality and morality is not an absolute novelty, but the awakening of something slumbering within us—an awakening through a *prise de conscience*, through reflection. In its own way, this awakening is testimony to universal providence against a philosophical Manicheanism, which saw a radical duality in the universe, the cohabitation of two alien principles, which, through a strange contradiction, made the life of spirit and consciousness spring from their impossible interaction.

But what is this latent morality in our nature, this grace deposited in the state enveloping our nature? Here is the secret of the enigmatic, unresolvable presence of the universal in the particular, a presence not resolvable to the eye of our intelligence. This total presence in us is an aspiration for the absolute; this aspiration is installed at the heart of our desire whose ground is Love. Therefore it is an insight into the nature of desire that has to introduce us to the unity of nature and the absolute. But for this to happen, it is necessary to shift from a mechanistic conception of nature to a dynamic one. This dynamism, so obscure on the ground of knowing, takes on its full meaning on that of action: striving and effort serve to mediate between what is and what ought to be, for what is fundamental is not what is already realized but what points to being [*tend à l'être*]; and what points to being is the absolute itself.

A Pauline vision of the universe, consisting of forces in tension, a world that longs for perfection. In being, there is more than what exists, what is given; there is the future. This is what constitutes desire. Desire, which is an attachment to being, is also a progress in being; in it, we recognize Spinoza's "conatus." In this desire, there is more than in egoism; there is love unaware of itself, "for desire always infinitely surpasses the determined limits of these objects. There is a disproportion between what these objects will justify for desire through the given reality, and what they really provoke. . . . What is active in these beings in being conscious of them is only desire, but in the absolute, it is love."[32] Therefore there is "an obscure love at the bottom of desire, which is God within us."[33]

It looks as though we may end up sanctifying everything in nature, in the name of this presence of the absolute in nature, and that the separation between egoism and love fades away: "What absolutely accounts for the effort through which each being tends to preserve in its being, in attaching itself to other objects, is that the being of these objects and that being's own object are one, and that at bottom, in each being it is being itself that loves itself through an eternal love."[34] In the absolute there is no desire that, unbeknown to itself, would not be love, and we are close to a Hegelian way of stating things: everything real is rational; evil is only a ruse the idea uses to realize itself. The egoist is not mistaken about the way things go, but he has not understood everything his egoism entails, or the implicit love of the absolute within it. Love gives depth to egoism. What must be said is that in the absolute, God loves himself even in our egoism. In the absolute, his love "consists in the identity of egoism and disinterest through the absolute positing of reality, the whole value to which egoism attaches itself in the absolute."[35] Things had to end up here: it is the ultimate consequence of the monism of Being, of a radical pantheism.

But is nature truly absorbed into the ideal? Unfortunately this is true only in the absolute. Everything that is, is in God; Being is everywhere present. But our point of view is not that of the absolute; it is at least distinct from God's point of view. There is a place within us for illusion: the illusion of an egoism unaware of itself as love. And this suffices to prevent the final absorption of nature into the ideal, of egoism into Love. And this also suffices to make the moral life a choice, an alternative between God and something else.

Here is where these philosophies, those of Lagneau and Lachelier, break down: nothing is that is not in God, and yet there is something in us that is an illusion, an error, evil.

We have seen this fatal contradiction on the level of theoretical reason: the being of Thought supports the whole approach, and yet "there is no more resemblance between divine understanding and human understanding, as we understand it, than between the dog constellation and a barking dog."[36] And it is a pantheist who says this. Everything gets reduced to the absolute, except our point of view, except the appearance inherent to our understanding. If it is true that nature is fundamentally one with God, its opposite is appearance and illusion. But is this illusion one with God? How could it be born within the fundamental purity of the Whole?

Practical philosophy runs aground on this same rock. Far from surmounting the antithesis, it deepens it. Absolutely speaking, egoism must be said to be love. It must be since "what ought to be gets confounded with what is."[37] Negation of evil, absolute quietism, is where an absolute pantheism leads. But what then? How can it be that our ultimate outcome should be a choice, an alternative? Is there something therefore that is and that ought not to be? Calling it non-Being to satisfy our identity of Being and Duty is satisfactory only as language. If we say that evil is nothingness, that our choice is between something and nothing—and these are the thinker's final words: "Chaos is nothing. To be or not to be, a self and everything, it is necessary to choose."[38] But how can egoism be a thing for human beings? The problem is only displaced. We do not have to break with true nature, which is God, but with appearance, which, at least, is not God. Moral life therefore remains a rupture, a sacrifice, a renouncement. Lagneau undoubtedly is correct: it is taking a stand not against the true laws of nature but against the apparent laws that make us believe that our individuality is the center of everything and of the universe of phenomena, what feeds our desires. So what it is necessary to surmount is: the desire that turns itself into illusion, and it is this illusion that is radical evil. It is this illusion that digs the ditch between egoism and love. Without a doubt, what has to be understood is desire, for "if desire were perfectly understood, it would deny itself as egotistical, and make itself disinterested."[39] But, precisely, to comprehend desire is to renounce the illusion of the egoist interpretation. To comprehend oneself is to choose, for there is within us our true reality, which is being, and our apparent reality, which is not. The ultimate choice is not between the absolute and nature but between Being and non-Being: "At each instant, the act through which every being constitutes itself is the affirmation of other people, of one's identity with everyone else, this is the starting point of our true reality and our apparent reality."[40] Moral life therefore will be "the perpetual abandoning by every being of its apparent reality which is the result of what it undergoes, that is, of what is not truly it."[41] Insofar as there is non-Being within us, something is but ought not to be—the moral life is renouncement, rupture, abandon, dying as oneself, sacrifice. It is necessary to lose oneself as appearance in order to discover oneself as being.

But what, then, will explain the genesis of the bad will, which adds the error of practical illusion to that of theoretical illusion and includes within itself non-Being? Another philosopher—Le Roy—will say that the bad will, insofar as it has any energy, borrows its impulse from the good will, which is God, and turns against its source. But where does the extreme malice of this turn come from? Not-Being, but this is what our turn amounts to.

Perhaps here we have one of the most basic antinomies of philosophy—and I do not believe any philosophy escapes it. A philosophy worthy of the name is a philosophy of Being, but moral philosophy is a philosophy of an alternative. A philosophy of Being is a philosophy of the One, a moral philosophy, a philosophy of duality.

Here I ask myself whether the personalist view might not attenuate the difficulty. Perhaps evil is linked to the autonomy of persons, and responsibility rests entirely in a creature's free act?

* * *

Moral life has revealed to us, with all its severity, a non-Being, which we can grasp only negatively, as an anti-thought, a scandal, chaos: an incommensurability that excludes every comparison, which does not stand in an external relation to Being, or have degrees, for there is no common measure between Being and non-Being.

There is more: moral life again reveals that Love does not fully express the unity that is the form of God. It is only a deficient approximation, a symbol. Our nature includes some non-Being, in that it includes illusion—but also in that there is Being in it; the absolute is never fully realized there, but only an effort toward unity. We must not say that unity is given in nature in the form of love, but that it *becomes*.

That Love cannot realize unity is easy to comprehend, for "love entails the complete identification of the loving subject and the loved object, an identification that will never be fully realized in nature, for then the subject would be grounded in its object, which is to say that there would no longer be Love."[42] Love exists only to the degree that the measure of or tendency toward unification leaves outside itself a certain margin of duality: "Two in one," is what Love necessarily is.

A profound insight; but must we conclude, with Lagneau, that "Love cannot exist" on the pretext that it cannot reach unity?[43] Perhaps it would be better to say that Love does not include precisely a pure and simple unity but implies the maximum of diversity in the maximum of unity. What,

I believe, is illusory is not the diversity of beings but the search for the world's absoluteness in a dead unity. In the society of persons, the ideal is not the dissolution of individuality but a reciprocal inwardness that brings to its maximum each one's originality. The most adequate concept of love would therefore be not unity, but communion. If one envisages Love from the angle of unity, it will be necessary to say, with Lagneau, that "fully realized, it no longer is Love."[44]

Making sense of the notion of Person would avoid, I believe, this paradox that Love tends to destroy itself. It is this conclusion, moreover, that follows from any unilateral analysis of spirits' assimilating themselves to one another. The world of spirits goes equally in the direction from homogeneous to heterogeneous, as from heterogeneous to homogeneous. Only going toward unity would lead to eliminating spirit. It is only within a collective consciousness that we may find this unity which is not communion. This is not where Love leads. The life of spirits creates diversity and unity in reciprocal proportions.

If so, for a philosophy like that of Lagneau, who seeks God as absolute in nature, Love necessarily remains inadequate for this unity. The diversity found there is not perfection but impotence. Even through Love, the absolute is not realized in mankind; and there remains a certain transcendence within immanence, a certain distance between the degrees of Being.

Immanence: for if the One lacks reality, no explanation can be given. Transcendence: for whatever concept of God we form, "God will not be, if the concept is exhaustive, that is, if it is merely a concept."

Therefore there is no expression fully adequate to God. One cannot even say that God is Love. This is just the least inadequate concept, for, owing to the plurality inherent to Love, we will be led, by equating Love and God, to introduce the relative into the absolute. When we say

> God loves himself with an eternal love, we imply in this way that God stands opposed to himself, loves himself in something other than himself, that he loves himself consequently on the condition of a nature different than his nature. We do not conceive God's love independently of every relation with the natures that depend on him; God can love himself, but only on the condition that he can be found in different natures; in other words, Love presupposes a duality, even a trinity, that is, an action starting from one nature and aiming at an end. . . . Through the very fact that Love exists, a multiplicity is posited in unity. . . . God can only love himself in other beings than himself. Love therefore has unity and constitutes it; but only on the

condition of diversity. Absolute Love can only consist in creating itself through creating others.[45]

Is this diversity of Being for Lagneau the true structure of the Universe or a necessary illusion of our understanding, a still insufficient comprehension of unity? This is perhaps one of the most difficult points to interpret in what Lagneau says; I think every statement about diversity, for Lagneau, must be placed on a symbolic level. Transcendence always remains an incomplete comprehension of immanence; it is truth to our measure, a dividedness inherent to our incurably divisive and never-unifying point of view.

The closing pages of Lagneau's book bear witness to this interpretation; in the search for the most adequate symbols of divine unity, tendency, effort, and action are introduced as middle terms between static Being and its diversity, on the one hand, and the absolute unity of existing beings on the other: "Every particular reality is an action."[46] This action is called appetite, desire, willing, depending on the degree of consciousness it illuminates. At first sight, one might think we have here a substitution for philosophy; one might believe that unity remains an ideal end, a limit, and that the last word of philosophy would be that being becomes, not that being is. In this sense, Love, which is an effort and a becoming, could well be the ground of Being.

But to Lagneau's way of thinking, the unity toward which the universe tends is not merely a possible, ideal, or virtual end of some tendency. That would be to abolish his earlier monism. In developing, nature does not create anything. It discovers itself: acting is not tending toward something that at present is nothing: "Action supposes the possibility of attaining its end, which supposes a reality. What is possible, compossible, is reality itself. Action is nothing other than the development of total reality in the individual Being. . . . Universal reality, alone, is what is truly given."[47]

These statements sound like Spinoza—but undoubtedly have a different implication. They signify, I believe, that the point of view of development in no way is a substituting of a philosophy of becoming for a philosophy of being, that there is no absolute creation in Bergson's sense of novelty, no radical becoming—simply an unfolding of the absolute, a passage from the implicit to the explicit. There is nothing new in the universe, simply deeper realities. Our progressive enrichments, our conquests are not inventions, but greater consciousness of our pre-possessions.

Therefore there is no need to see in these last pages the birth of a new point of view, for which God *becomes* in the Heraclitean sense of the word. Our becoming is situated in relation to realized being. It is true to say that through Love and its effort toward unity God ceaselessly *becomes* in the world. But God *becomes* because he is. Becoming is an effort to mimic Being. Between becoming and Being there is a symbolic relationship. But it seems to me that this symbolic relation, implicitly affirmed in these pages by Lagneau, is nothing other than true transcendence, the true distance between God and the world. Is this not what this statement by Lagneau implies: "The true cause of the evolution of beings is the feeling they have of the unity of the universe, of which they are a part, and the affirmation that—*this unity which is given independently of them*[48]—they can indefinitely continue to realize within themselves."[49]

Reading Lagneau therefore leads to an insistence on the point of view of transcendence. It is only from this angle that we can conceive both that being is and that being becomes. To some degree, it is necessary to deny the univocity of being. If God is one with the world, the conception of being as action and becoming abolishes a philosophy of the absolute. If we conceive that God may be, in some way, distinct from the world—a distinction that must not be thought of spatially and is only a difference in perfection and moral value—we can say that being exists "under" being, although held up only by it.

Still, we should honor Lagneau for having recalled the ruinous fate of every pure doctrine of transcendence. We cannot place ourselves straightaway within transcendence. It must first be delivered to us in a presence, an obscure appetite, a need. This is the love that is God in us, which the psalmist sings of: "As a deer longs for flowing streams."[50] Anticipated love, "God can only love himself by creating, signifying that absolute love must consist in God's creation of himself through creating others."[51] But is this diversity of God and world, as Lagneau believes, a lack of comprehension, an incompleteness in our thinking; must we not say that God is something even beyond Love? And why would this not be the true face of the universe?

What is more, if the ideal of metaphysics is to comprehend the unity of Being, ought we not to welcome the failure of metaphysics, for this failure marks the place for moral philosophy? Because our nature always falls short of God—because there is in Being something that ought not to be, effort has a meaning, we are called on to sacrifice, and an alternative drives us forward. Moral effort, action that ceaselessly struggles against the slippery slope of a bad will, lives in this gap that metaphysics cannot fill between God and nature: because there is not-Being, our nature must be a renouncement and a sacrifice, because God is not, through our effort God must become. The moral life is an *alternative* to the degree that the *monism* of metaphysics is incomplete. For Hegel, there is no alternative. Chaos is nothing real, yet "to be or not to be, oneself and everything, one must choose."[52]

Conclusion
The Method of Immanence and the Doctrine of Immanence

The goal of these concluding pages is to bring together and orient the few critical remarks made during the course of my analysis. I have tried to unite them around the idea of immanence. I must say that this critique is largely inspired by the doctrines of Maurice Blondel.

Lachelier's and Lagneau's philosophies are essentially an effort to make a method of immanence coincide with a philosophy of immanence—that is, to make the existence of God coincide with the very effort to reach him: "Philosophy is total reality, that is, if we understand this properly, universal reason gaining consciousness of an accounting for itself" (Lachelier).

"God reaches himself in the very act through which we posit any thought as true" (Lagneau).

I do not believe that a method of immanence necessarily implies a philosophy of immanence. More: I do not believe that a method of immanence is sufficient by itself. All the more so, a philosophy of immanence, if it is not to be wrong, remains radically incomplete.

A. The Method of Immanence

1. The Necessity of a Method of Immanence

Lachelier and Lagneau should be praised for having recalled that there is really only one problem: that of God. Every partial problem is just arbitrarily taken from the totality of the problem of God. Everything is within the Whole. Hence, the normal starting point for inquiry into God will be an inventorying of all his possessions. This is the central ideal of the reflexive method. That there is or is not a transcendence is not something one can immediately begin from. The thing-in-itself transcendent to our spirit is so far removed from the vicissitudes of our phenomenal existence that it is always beyond human reach. Lachelier said: things only begin to exist for us when we know we are cognizant of them. The same thing applies to God. It is normal to being analyzing our Whole innerness. But the problem is knowing if we reach total truth through simply dividing up a prior formed tangle, by simply passing from the implicit to the explicit.

Before turning to the very idea of something foreign to our inner possessions, let us look at where these latter lead us. I believe that reflection consists more in discovering within ourselves absences than presences. This is an idea dear to Lagneau, and I believe that here, as in many other points, if Lachelier is more precise, Lagneau is more insightful. We deepen our understanding only because at each level we find something lacking. Sensation lacks something; we sense that our task is to determine what it is, to disengage the maximum of intelligibility regarding it. We sense that it is necessary to add to sensation the necessity it lacks. There is also something lacking in a purely intellectual truth, and this is one, and not the least, of the benefits that Lagneau has demonstrated: the futility of every philosophy grounded on self-evidence, from Cartesianism to positivism. Here lies even the root of a true atheism: intellectual satisfaction, suturing understanding with clear and distinct ideas is the real obstacle to further research. This negative method is much more insightful than the positive method that Lachelier develops starting from his *Cours de Logique* through his "Psychology and Metaphysics." It is an essentially dry-boned, impoverished method. Did not Lachelier judge it so himself when he said that this formal God would be radically indeterminant and maybe chimeric, if he does not show himself through some fact that is at the same time an act of caritas?

But, if something is lacking with sensation and understanding, what must be said is that something is also lacking for a purely speculative approach. Here is where Lagneau's superiority over Lachelier is his having recalled that if the problem of God is the whole problem, the search for God embraces our whole life both as practical and as theoretical.

2. Reflection and Action

We are indebted to Lagneau for having set us on guard against the illusion of a purely speculative search for the truth. Our progress in being is not just progress in awareness, speculative progress; or to put it another way, for there to be progress in consciousness, it cannot simply be progress made through speculation.

Lachelier was correct when he said: "we affirm ourselves to be such as we are; but on the other hand we are that which we affirm ourselves to be." But we have just one way to affirm ourselves, through reflection as realization. As Lagneau puts it: "Philosophy is first the search for reality through reflection, and next its realization. Action therefore is not, as Lachelier says, an application, a corollary. The corollary applies to the general assertion. If the goal of cognition is to make our explicit knowledge equal to all our pre-possessions, to our whole implicit knowledge—to expand our consciousness, we must turn to action, for in realizing what we know we increase our knowledge, and through it, our being: "If the disposition to love, to bind oneself to universal being, independent of our sensibility or our individuality, may vanish into the one we are, intellectual life would also disappear. Most definitely, we have, at each moment, the certainty we deserve. . . . The meaning of things appears more clearly to us to the degree that we increase our own value" (Lagneau).

The least of our actions includes an infinite knowledge. As Lagneau will say, the least effort of a good will *realizes* the most chimeric of philosophies—realizes, that is, not simply applies, but rather makes things pass from a more or less utopian possibility to a concrete state of life. Through our action, the ideal *validates* itself, and also *is*, because to some degree it has succeeded in shaping nature. We seek in vain, in a purely speculative order, the bond between nature and the ideal; action confirms, by being a fact, what speculation can merely explain: nature is not foreign to the ideal, because it is its point of application and matter. But it is true that one must have the courage to act, and this is not merely cognitive—and one must be able to profit from one's action, and in this way, action is a call for further reflection. So knowledge cut off from its practical prolongation sinks into the shifting sand of what is possible and abstract—blind action becomes drunk on anarchical romanticism or turns into the most servile conformism.

Cognition that is a call to action, an action that is a reason for further thought—this is the true cycle, or rather cycloid, of philosophy, "this alternative propulsion, like that of a wheel turning as it advances," which must not "complete itself as a circle."[1]

Yet someone may say: if action really adds something to knowledge, is there necessarily within it something perfectly blind, an act of faith, a risk that must be taken, which precisely is the fringe of what it does not yet know before its being realized? Yes and no: yes, in the sense that action adds something to our explicit knowledge; no, in the sense that action *realizes*—that is, again not simply applies, but incorporates itself into, adds to being—what was known only implicitly, what was simply a premonition.

But it is true, Lagneau does want to take us further. He sees something else in action. Action makes explicit not just an implicit knowledge, which one first grants, through a preliminary act of trust—action *creates* the Whole that is our knowledge; it *grounds* our certainty. Our being continually undoes itself; ceaselessly falls into habits and unconsciousness; it is constantly necessary to unleash it, through an inner creation, to turn back from the slippery slope leading to egoism, cowardliness, chaos, nonbeing. We must not just undergo Being, we must *make* it.

Must we push the responsibility for our thoughts and our action this far? Must we bear the full weight of absolute thought? Is what is at stake in the alternative between a good will and egoism, in the choice between the courage to live life and cowardliness Thought as a Whole? Do we really make Being through our thinking and our action?—or is the human problem not a problem at our own level, that is, a modest collaboration in a larger, overall work? For my part, I believe that it is necessary to be modest: we do not have it within us to *create* Being, but rather in some way to *receive* it. The drama of the universe is played out in other natures than just our own. We not only have to make our life, but we must also in a way welcome it. We must not only develop our inner resources, by making the implicit explicit, we must open ourselves to external resources, expand our human reality, in contact with other partial realities.

3. Reflection and Reception

Some philosophies have imagined that the role of thought was passively to reflect Being, wholly constituted outside of this thought. Man, the mirror of things, need only abandon himself quietly to the solicitations coming from the outside. No more responsibility, no more anxiety either. In truth, no one has completely gone all the way in this direction, for it is easier, for cognition, to suppress known things (absolute idealism) than the knowing subject (absolute realism); but I believe that this extreme opposition indicates to us the exaggeration of a philosophy that would make man bear the whole weight for certainty. In the universe, there are collaborations. Beings have need of one another, and it would be vain to want to draw everything from human thought. We must not just dig deeper; we must open ourselves.

Let us start from the humblest of such beginnings. The philosophies of Lachelier and Lagneau have shown to a large degree that it is illusory to want to draw matter from knowledge of its form. Always, on the human scale, this is a utopian claim. There is a minimum of trust that must be granted to what is not us. This minimum of trust dispenses us from the maximum of creation which is not up to us. We ought to be humble: we do not have to carry the whole weight of the universe. Our responsibility does not extend that far; we need things in order to be ourselves. And we do not create these things. They constitute a true otherness for thinking. Above all we should not be scandalized by this commerce with the material universe. Lachelier and Lagneau have shown this to be fruitful. One of the merits of the reflexive method is that it reminds us that in being dependent on things we can rediscover ourselves. Thinking, before any contact with the universe, is empty and impoverished: "Thinking is the truth, and the truth is in the things themselves. That is where spirit must look if it wants to find itself, and one can say of it, in the words of the Gospel, that it only finds itself by losing itself" (Lachelier).

"Again, our interior life is not sufficient by itself, it must look outside itself and draw on the universe before reflecting on its own existence or representing it to itself" (Lagneau).

We must never lose touch with this welcoming, this initial trust; we must accept a radical realism without any regrets. Matter is not a scandal, for it presides over thought's early stages.

Nothing can be further from us, beyond this, than the idea that this trust can dispense us from thinking: for it is not a question of becoming all things but of internalizing them: thinking completes the being of things, it unwraps all that is virtual, it "analyzes" them in every aspect: thinking does create something; what is more, it is necessary to say that this work, far from being a forgery, is normal. It is the very mission of thinking to analyze the real, then to recreate it in terms of still richer, more concentrated intuitive syntheses; in this sense, thinking fulfills being, thinking is about being. But we must recognize that our creations are necessarily based on something that does not come from us. This is the most elementary collaboration of human thought with what is other than it.

We seek in order to find God, but we seek by finding the world; is it not to this Augustinian formula—which Blondel likes so much—that the reflexive method leads us: *Ab exterioribus ad interiora, ub interioribus ad superiora?*

There is more: this welcoming reception, which begins on the level of things, is not complete there. Science does not answer all our desires, and we have other latent rich sources to develop. More precisely, a new world offers itself for our discovery: the world of persons. Love is this higher search and reception. Here again, it is Lagneau who showed us this in all its richness. But an equivocation runs through his whole analysis because he misses its essential basis, the notion of a person. If we understand, as needs to be shown, that persons are in some way all distinct from one another, loving means going outside oneself, discovering an alterity, internalizing others by externalizing oneself. To be sure, we must agree with Lagneau that "in the absolute each particular being exists only through its identity with all others, within Being as a whole"—but to get there "from ourselves to ourselves, we have to go out before reentering."[2]

I believe we have to take this expression in an absolutely realist sense: the reality of others is really distinct from my own. I discover our identity only along the way of our differences. For a second time, philosophy is not just reflection, but a welcoming. For a second time, discovering the absolute is not a simple uncovering of our pre-possessions, a simple passing from the implicit to the explicit, but an expanding of our being through the intrusion of some alterity. It is through collaboration with the other that we discover the same, that we realize our own depth.

Is that all? I do not believe so; perhaps there is still a whole universe to explore beyond our commerce with things and other people. Perhaps there is a supreme welcome, a highest love, that draws us outside ourselves—and for some, outside all their prior possessions. Perhaps there is an ultimate dispossession that finally makes us coincide with our prior possession. Man's prayer, God's grace—this is the final encounter that man must perhaps make in order to complete his wisdom and fulfill his philosophy. Is this what Lachelier calls faith—I mean what is given for human reflection, which is perhaps the other, what they have experienced? Yes, but not completely so. For faith in his *Notes on Pascal's Wager* is a hope, its modality is possibility; perhaps the final exploration takes place in the totally concrete, in the fullness of being. This would be the supreme reality, this time more than ever in the realist sense of the word, the most filled with alterities.

The priests who like to distinguish orders will call this confusion: they would like to juxtapose the closed world of philosophy and the pure world of faith—whose jurisdiction they usually place under some sovereign authority that will have charge over reflection; as though, truly, the supernatural, in fulfilling the natural, does not enter the cycle of reflection and of philosophy, as though the thinker's task were not to embrace the totality of his explorations in a personal and responsible reflection.

B. The Doctrine of Immanence

1. The Necessity of a Doctrine of Transcendence

There can be no doubt that a reflective method must be based on a prospective method, that a method of immanence must be nourished by welcoming some transcendence. The philosophical problem is knowing whether God is strictly identical with our reflection, or with the completed reflection of all our explorations. I believe that immanence, to be true, remains incomplete, that there is a doctrine of transcendence internal to the doctrine of immanence. We need to be clear about this term. The hypothesis of transcendence consists in recognizing between God and the world, and even between God and our reason, a special distinction which is not that of some spatial exteriority. Transcendence is not opposed to immanence as external to internal, but as diversity to monism and pantheism.

Can there be a doctrine of transcendence? Lachelier does not believe so, for if there is a doctrine, it must be that of immanence; and if there is transcendence, it is not the object of any doctrine but a wager, a hope, faith:

> Pantheism, it seems to me, first assumes the unity of being, then that this being is at bottom spiritual, reason, even freedom, although initially unaware of itself, but destined to appear to itself in the end, in the form of thought. I believe there is no other being than this for pure philosophy and that it is essentially pantheist. But we can *believe* in a *beyond* the world, in the spiritual, but with no admixture of beings, not becoming, trans-real, and unknowable to us in our present conditions of existence. If we reserve for this beyond the name God, we will be content to call universal spiritual being the *world*; and in distinguishing in this way between the world and God, we will not be pantheist.[3]

From his side, Lagneau does not say that there is a transcendence of God to the world. The ideal of reason is, for him as for Lachelier, the identity of nature and God, the unity of being.

I believe that, without denying the unity of being, it is necessary to affirm degrees of being; this affirmation follows from the very failure of pantheism.

Let us think about the absorption of the sensible world: for Lachelier it becomes an unsolvable problem, once it is weakened in his eyes to having the status of being a symbol. He was led to making the ideal of reason a matter of faith. Lagneau, for his part, seeks a fuller identity, an integral monism: but he could not satisfy this demand except by accusing the understanding of illusion and error, something Lachelier never did. The problem of the absorption of the sensible world in God thus comes down for Lagneau to the reduction of human understanding to being God.

Therefore there is an essential inability to totally reduce nature to being God. Is there something scandalous about this? No, not if we think that matter is, as we have seen above, an aid for man, spirit's lowest degree of attenuation, which allows man to realize himself more fully in internalizing this thought which does not think itself. Perhaps a hierarchical concept of the universe can save us from this condemnation of matter, which is normally the antithetic result of its negation by monism: history shows us either wanting to absorb matter into the absolute, or rejecting it as a scandal. In reality, each degree of being is an occasion for finding a higher degree. Matter's destiny is to lead to the discovery of spirit. But it has to be thought of as a collaboration, not as an identity.

If now we turn to human reason, we find a deep disagreement between Lachelier and Lagneau; for the former, the structure of human reason is strictly one with God: human reason is God who grasps himself in us; to the degree that I think, it is universal thought thinking in me. For Lagneau, on the contrary, a certain powerlessness, a relative falsification is inherent to the understanding "which does not grasp reality as it is, but which disperses it in order to explain it." So it is necessary to say that "there is no more resemblance between divine and human understanding, as we understand it, than between the dog constellation and a barking dog."

Lagneau's position is a minimum; from Lachelier's point of view, one is obliged to reach it but to grant several distinctions between looking for God in man and within God himself. This inquiry unfolds over time. What is more, it does not all unfold on the same plane of purity; it is a conquest, a consolidation; the synthesis in "Psychology and Metaphysics" has to be interpreted in the same way. For our reflection, God becomes. But in reality God has no need to consolidate himself, because God is. Undoubtedly this existence of God, distinct from becoming and this effort, is not something external to our consciousness; he exists in us, in an implicit state, like something unconscious, and this suffices for transcendence not to contradict immanence. But the Unconscious is precisely what, within our very thinking, is a thought but not a thinking that thinks itself. But what then is the Unconscious? What makes it implicit if not the real and the transcendent? We gain nothing in calling the Unconscious what we do not want to call transcendence; within thinking we must grant a gap between *esse* and *percipi*. A thought that is but which is not known is a transcendent thought, however internal it may be to our being. It is our being inasmuch as this being is not Consciousness. So the very idea of passing from the implicit to the explicit includes the idea of transcendence.

Our reflection therefore is not God, and Lagneau put this well: our effort, our love, through which God unceasingly comes into the world, does not abolish the certainty that God is eternally completely perfect: "The true cause of the evolution of beings is the feeling they have of the unity of the universe, of which they speak, and the affirmation that this unity, which is given independently of them, is something they can infinitely work to realize more and more within themselves." Through our effort we unceasingly attempt to rejoin God, but the distance between our becoming and the fullness of being is genuine transcendence. As said above, in discussing Lagneau, a relative distinction between our effort and God allows preserving a meaning for becoming and for being. Were God to be this becoming, we would be faced with a creation lacking any orientation, a blind freedom, a nature that grows without following any rules; on the contrary, this becoming stands out against a background of being that overflows it, judges it, orients it. This becoming is an effort to realize a more complete nature, which already is and which is God.

But then what is this absolute that guides the relative? How is it given to us? What is this endpoint which is the reason for our effort? Lachelier gives us two answers: that of philosophy and that of faith: on the one hand, this endpoint is a pure idea, but so undetermined, so desubstantialized that it cannot provide the least meaning to life. On the other, our life's guide, the *esse* that orients our *fieri*, will be the object of a pure faith, which as not bound to the postulations of reason is purely gratuitous, unless it were to be a sheer fact of revelation. There is no middle term between the pure and empty idea and a living, gratuitous faith. Undoubtedly there is a contradiction between these two ways of conceiving God: but precisely because they are totally disproportionate and not juxtaposable, there is no reason to give them the same name.

Do we find a more unified idea of God in Lagneau, an idea that participates both in the richness of the God of faith and the certainty of the formal God? To the degree that Lagneau's answer is not purely agnostic, we have this response; two ideas express the existence of God, unity and love; but the second one is a living realization of the first one. This living God is truly the development of the formal God, because love is what unifies. But I believe that we do not find the fullness of God in Lagneau except insofar as he breaks the rigid framework of intellectualism: God is given through an obscure need, grace that slumbers in our nature, love that sleeps at the bottom of our desire, a nostalgia for God. If we push further in this direction, which is quite close to Blondel's point of view, it would be necessary to say that the true guide of our becoming, of our intellectual and moral effort lies in this pre-possession, this anticipation, this implicit knowledge slumbering in the obscurest regions of our crystalized clear ideas. Life and action are less clear but richer than our pure ideas. But it would then be necessary to admit that we have broken the framework of intellectualism, as we have seen since our opening pages, the intellectualism which postulates that every richness to come is already contained in the zone of our clear and distinct ideas. Every norm is there, in our explicit knowledge; it suffices to expand our surface knowledge, which gains nothing in depth thereby. Perhaps, on the contrary, this obscure knowledge, which slumbers on the fringe of our soul, in that halo not yet absorbed through reflection, and which is life, action—contains norms, and even a veritable natural revelation, a deep-lying will that signifies something decisive about our fate. This point which Lachelier so strongly resists is one that Lagneau moves toward.

This is the profound being that can guide our development; it lies within us, and our whole life consists in sorting out our explicit possessions and our implicit pre-possessions. It is what Blondel calls uneasiness. This transcendence is an internal inadequation, a distance within ourself: "Prior to every speculative prejudice, what is given us is neither fixed nor mobile; it is neither the relative nor the absolute; it is what Malebranche called 'unease'—a state of perpetual instability or an intimate disproportion, such that each attempt to satisfy the prior demands that manifest themselves spontaneously to thought reveal even further demands which impose themselves in a moral way on action."[4]

2. Transcendence and Personalism

God's transcendence over man only plainly appears with the perspective of a philosophy of the Person. To be sure, my thinking participates in universal thought (always the immanence that supports transcendence), but it remains truly distinct only because thinking is the act of a person, and in general an act that can be only that of a person. A person is essentially a focal point for acts: the act of intellectual cognition, of love, of repulsion, of the will. The person is the supra-conscious intersection of his acts (supra-conscious: we cannot know the person other than by analyzing him; this is not a mistake but a necessity—and even an enriching necessity, for we grasp no unity other than through the concentrating of points of view).

This connection of the notion of an act to that of a person is essential. Every philosophy that argues against the doctrine of concepts and that seeks to substitute that of judgment, of the lived activity of thinking— reaches its goal only if it renounces impersonalism. One says *cogito*, not *cogitate*. An impersonal act makes no sense, and in any case impersonalism leads to substantializing thinking, turning it into an object. We need to convince ourselves of this: what, in thought, is impersonal is the subject, the judgment. Above, it was said that a re-absorbing of the concept into the judgment, of the object into the act is impossible, that thinking necessarily appears as the tension between two functions: thinking and the thought, *cogito et cogitata*.

Here is perhaps the meaning of this opposition: thinking is the personal face of what is thought, judgment, what distinguishes minds; the thought is the impersonal face of thinking, what unites minds, impersonal mind. Perhaps because we cannot renounce the personality or the impersonality of thinking is why it is impossible to reduce it to an object-function and a subject-function, to a concept and a judgment. But this is a purely personal hypothesis. For this hypothesis, the profound meaning of these philosophies would be to bet on both an impersonal philosophy and a philosophy of judgment, of the subject, of the act—which can happen only through a criss-crossing of the two functions of thinking. We would reach the same conclusions through an analysis of the notion of freedom, which cannot be attributed to impersonal thought and which, like an act of thinking, is essentially bound to thought about a person.

If so, if our thinking is like this, we cannot say that God is human thinking, for 1. our act of thought is not God's act. An "I think" is irreducible to "God thinks," for it would be necessary to reduce them both to the hybrid intermediary of an "it thinks." Transcendence that in no way negates the true interiority of thinking finds its true basis in personalism; 2. on the other hand, human thinking through its double function does not realize divine unity. In God, the personal and impersonal function must be grounded in a higher synthesis. It is certain that God is truth, but it is no less certain that he is a Person. If it is true that all our progress takes place through an increasing unity with other minds, and also through an intensification of our personal originality, the Person is the world's highest interest and God is the principle of the Person as much as of unity. For us the synthesis of impersonality and personality, of truth and love, of the norm and the creative *Fiat* is incomprehensible.

3. Degrees of Being and Nonbeing

God's transcendence over the human person takes on its meaning when one sets man back into the universe. In him is realized a movement that outlines every degree of being. If we envisage the relations between persons, and no longer of God to mankind, we must not talk about the life of the mind but about the life of minds. There is a society of minds; this leads to a monadism. No doubt this diversity and this pluralism need to be better understood. If we seem to be in the world of numbers and arithmetic, we are not in the world of space. Proof of this is that this distinction in no way suppresses a true interiority of minds. Love touches my inner me only by passing through others. The unity and diversity of minds are also essential to Love: a total fusion of persons would create a collective consciousness and not the communion that creates diversity and unity in equal proportions.

This communion is the culmination of a latent tendency throughout the universe. This diversity of minds exists in every degree of the world. It is illusory to seek matter as the absolute unity; yes, there is unity in the world: determinism expresses this, but determinism is a unilateral point of view. Diversity runs even down to matter.

In internalizing the universe through thought, man is not just seeking unity. The mind's task is not solely to assemble the many into the one. On the contrary, our faculties of analysis must multiply to the maximum the aspects of the universe, and true unity is to be sought above, in an intuition that would be a concentration of as many points of view as analysis has been able to reach.

We see outlined then throughout the universe that communion of minds which is creative of variety and unity. In this way we are led to envisage degrees of being, where, with more or less perfection, a dense, multicolored concentration is realized.

Should we go still further? Should we say that not only are there degrees of being, but also of nonbeing? Evil is an unsolvable problem for Lachelier, and Lagneau's monism finally bifurcates into a moral alternative: being or notbeing.

I wonder whether impersonalism is not responsible for this; maybe evil is tied to our personal autonomy; maybe evil is uniquely the fruit of freedom and a personal task. We often confuse the problem of suffering and that of evil: the former is a universal problem, the latter a human problem. Suffering is not evil, nor is death, for biological individuality has no *right* to life. That the wolf devours the lamb is neither good nor bad, and this is just as indifferent as the ivy's sucking the oak's sap. If suffering seems an evil, it is because we implicitly assign the dignity of being a person to the animal, and to the human animal. Suffering is a biological necessity. The general success of life is all that counts, whatever the individual sacrifices may be. It is only in the world of persons that each unit has an infinite value and must not be sacrificed to the whole. On the contrary, evil does pose a problem; but evil is the deed of a person and a product of freedom. The problem of evil is totally unsolvable for a monism, pantheism, and impersonalism.

There are degrees of being, but not of nonbeing.

Why, then, is the absolute not all that is? How are we to comprehend the movement that leads from God to the world? We do see in any case that the perspective of transcendence will be God's prerogative distinct from our reflection. God's ways are not our ways.

Notes

Foreword
1. Paul Ricoeur, "Jean Nabert: Une Relecture," in Philippe Capelle-Dumont, *Jean Nabert et la Question du Divin* (Paris: Cerf, 2003), 141–53.

Preface
1. Paul Ricoeur, "Philosophie et prophétisme," in *Lectures 3* (Paris: Seuil, 1993), 154.
2. Paul Ricoeur, "Intellectual Autobiography," trans. Kathleen Blamey, in Lewis Edwin Hahn, ed., *The Philosophy of Paul Ricoeur* (Chicago and LaSalle, IL: Open Court, 1995), 6.
3. Ibid.
4. Paul Ricoeur, *Oneself as Another*, trans. Kathleen Blamey (Chicago: University of Chicago Press, 1992), 34.
5. Paul Ricoeur, *From Text to Action: Essays in Hermeneutics II*, trans. Kathleen Blamey and John B. Thompson (Evanston: Northwestern University Press, 1991), 12.
6. Jean Greisch, "L'Herméneutique *More Gallico Demonstrata*," in Jean-François Mattéi, ed., *Philosopher en Français: Langue de la Philosophie et Langue Nationale* (Paris: Presses Universitaires de France, 2001), 59–82.
7. Jean Nabert, "La philosophie réflexive," in idem., *L'Expérience Intérieure de la Liberté et Autres Essais de Philosophie Morale* (Paris: Presses Universitaires de France, 1994), 397–411.
8. Ibid., 404.
9. Paul Ricoeur, *Gabriel Marcel and Karl Jaspers: Philosophie du mystère et philosophie de paradoxe* (Paris: Temps Présent, 1947).

10. Jules Lachelier, *Du fondement de l'induction*, suivi de *Psychologie et Métaphysique* et de *Notes sur le pari de Pascal* (Paris: Félix Alcan, 1924), 170; "Psychology and Metaphysics," in *The Philosophy of Jules Lachelier*, trans. Edward G. Ballard (The Hague: Martinus Nijhoff, 1960), 94–95.

11. See the report from the first *Congrès International de philosophie* in the *Revue de Métaphysique et de Morale* 8:5 (1900): 566–619.—translator's note.

12. Paul Ricoeur, *Freedom and Nature: The Voluntary and the Involuntary*, trans. Erazim V. Kohák (Evanston: Northwestern University Press, 1966), 15.

13. Jean Nabert, *Le Désire de Dieu* (Paris: Aubier-Montaigne, 1966).

14. Johann Gottlieb Fichte, *The Way Toward the Blessed Life: or, The Doctrine of Religion: Lectures Delivered at Berlin 1806*, trans. William Smith (London: John Chapman, 1849; Washington, DC: University Publications of America, 1977).

15. Paul Ricoeur, *The Conflict of Interpretations* (Evanston: Northwestern University Press, 1974), 328.

16. Ibid., 222.

17. Ibid., 329.

Introduction: Reflexive Method

1. Jules Lagneau, *De l'existence de Dieu* (Paris: Félix Alcan, 1925), vi.

2. Léon Brunschvicg, *L'Idéalisme contemporain* (Paris: Félix Alcan, 1921), 174.

3. Jules Lachelier, "*Du fondement de l'induction*" in *Œuvres de Jules Lachelier*, vol. 1 (Paris: Félix Alcan, 1933), 46; "The Foundation of Induction," in *The Philosophy of Jules Lachelier*, trans. Edward G. Ballard (The Hague: Martinus Nijhoff, 1960), 21.

4. Jules Lagneau, *De l'existence de Dieu* (Paris: Félix Alcan, 1935), 44.

5. Brunschvicg, *L'Idéalisme contemporaine*, 84.

6. Lachelier, "*Du fondement de l'induction*," 46/21.

7. Jules Lagneau, Fragment 10, *Écrits de Jules Lagneau*, réunis par les soins de ses disciples (Paris: Union pour la Vérité, 1925).

8. Ibid., Fragment 23.

9. Jules Lachelier, "Sur la morale positive," Société française de philosophie, 26 mars 1908, *Œuvres*, 2:157.

10. Jules Lachelier, "Sur le problème religieux et la dualité de la nature humaine," from the February 4, 1913, meeting of the *Société Française de Philosophie* (*Œuvres*, 2:167–71).

11. *Revue de Métaphysique et de Morale* 8 (1900): 570–75.

12. Henry Bergson, *Matter and Memory*, trans. N. M. Paul and W. S. Palmer (New York: Zone Books, 1991), 184–85.

13. Henry Bergson, *Creative Evolution*, trans. Arthur Miller (New York: Modern Library, 1944), 209–10.

14. Jules Lachelier, "*Psychologie et Métaphysique*," *Œuvres*, 1:207; "Psychology and Metaphysics," *Philosophy of Jules Lachelier*, 86–87.

15. Lachelier, *Du fondement de l'induction*, 37/7.
16. Ibid.
17. Ibid., 21/1.
18. Ibid.
19. "Réponse de J. Lachelier à M. Weber," *Bulletin de la Société Française de Philosophie* (1904), in *Œuvres* 2:127.
20. Fragment 13 (*Écrits de Jules Lagneau*, 304).
21. Ibid.
22. Brunschvicg, *L'Idéalisme contemporain*, 87.
23. Fragment 24 (*Écrits de Jules Lagneau*, 304).
24. Ibid.
25. Jules Lagneau, "Leçon sur le Judgment," in *Célèbres leçons* (Nîmes: Imprimerie coopérative La Laborieuse, 1926), 172.
26. Lachelier, *Psychologie et métaphysique* (*Œuvres*, 1:213/92).
27. Brunschvicg, *L'Idéalisme contemporain*, 185.
28. Lachelier, *Psychologie et métaphysique*, 217/95.
29. Lagneau, *De l'existence de Dieu*, 144.
30. Ibid., 152.
31. Ibid., 82.

Naturalism and the Problem of God
1. Jules Lachelier, *Du fondement de l'induction*, 21/1.
2. Ibid., 46/21.
3. Ibid., 47–48/22.
4. Ibid., 48/23.
5. Ibid.
6. Ibid., 52/25.
7. Ibid., 58–59/31.
8. Ibid., 64/35.
9. Ibid., 64/36.
10. Ibid., 68/37.
11. Ibid., 58/30.
12. Ibid., 47/22.
13. Ibid., 69/39–40.
14. Ibid., 92/56.
15. Ibid. 70/39–40.
16. Ibid., 74/42–43.
17. Ibid., 75/43.
18. Ibid., 82/48.
19. Ibid., 86/52.
20. Ibid., 78/46.
21. Ibid., 80/47.
22. Ibid., 81/48.
23. Ibid.

24. Ibid., 79/46.
25. Ibid., 79–80/47.
26. Ibid., 79/47.
27. Ibid., 76/44.
28. It is worth noting in passing the introduction of the notion of a symbol to attach a lower plane of thinking to a higher one. This notion will play a central role in the idealistic phases of Lachelier's thought.
29. Ibid., 80/47.
30. Jules Lachelier, "Philosophie," *Œuvres*, 2:204; *The Philosophy of Jules Lachelier*, 117.
31. Lachelier, *Du fondement de l'induction*, 53/26.
32. Ibid., 55/28.
33. Ibid.
34. Jules Lachelier, *Cours de Logique professé à l'École Normale Supérieur en 1876–1877: Leçon XVII, Du scepticisme*.
35. Ibid.
36. Lachelier, *Du fondement de l'induction*, 60/32.
37. Ibid., 77/44.
38. Ibid., 29–30.
39. Lachelier, *Cours de logique, Leçon VI: de l'Induction*.
40. Ibid.
41. Lachelier, *Fondement de l'induction*, 89/53.
42. Ibid., 89/54
43. Ibid., 90/55.
44. Ibid., 86/52.
45. Ibid., 87/52–53.
46. Ibid., 88/53.
47. Ibid., 92/56.
48. "Annotations au vocabulaire de la Société Française de Philosophie," *Œuvres*, tome II (Paris: Alcan, 1933), 204; *The Philosophy of Jules Lachelier*, 117.
49. Jules Lachelier, *Cours de Logique, Leçon XIV: des Lois morales*.
50. Note the surprising kinship of these remarks by Lachelier with those of Lagneau.

The Formal God or the Idea of God

1. Jules Lachelier, *Cours de logique, Leçon XVIII: De l'idéalisme*.
2. Jules Lachelier, "Psychologie et Métaphysique," *Œuvres*, 1:193/76.
3. Ibid., 200/88.
4. Ibid., 201/82. The will expresses itself, *symbolizes* itself through a feeling, and on the basis of perception.
5. Ibid., 194/76.
6. Ibid., 201/82.
7. Ibid.

8. Ibid., 201/83.
9. Ibid., 204/83.
10. Ibid., 206/86.
11. Ibid., 207/86.
12. Ibid.
13. Ibid., 219/96.
14. Ibid., 206/86.
15. Ibid., 208/87–88.
16. Maurice Blondel, *La Pensée* (Paris: Félix Alcan, PUF, 1934), 49.
17. The Latin word *esse* is spelled *essé* in this thesis—editor's note.
18. Lachelier, *Psychologie et Métaphysique*, 209/88.
19. Ibid.—translation altered.
20. Ibid.
21. Ibid., 209/88–89.
22. Ibid., 211/90.
23. Ibid., 209/83.
24. Ibid., 211/90.
25. Ibid., 210/89.
26. Ibid., 211/90.
27. Ibid.
28. Ibid., 211/90.
29. Ibid., 210/89.
30. Ibid.
31. Ibid.
32. Lachelier, *Du fondement de l'induction*, 80/47.
33. Lachelier, *Psychologie et Métaphysique*, 212/90.
34. Ibid.
35. Ibid.
36. Ibid., 212/91.
37. Ibid., 212/91.
38. Ibid., 213/91.
39. Ibid., 216/94.
40. Ibid., 213/91—translation altered.
41. Jules Lachelier, "Sur la Morale Positive," *Œuvres*, 2:157.
42. Lachelier, *Psychologie et Métaphysique*, 213/91.
43. Ibid.
44. Ibid.
45. Ibid., 213/92.
46. Ibid., 214/92.
47. Ibid., 217–18/99.
48. From the November 19, 1908, session of the French Society of Philosophy, "Science and Religion," *Oeuvres*, 2:161.
49. In his annotations to the vocabulary proposed by the French Society of Philosophy, "Science and Religion," *Oeuvres*, 2:215.

50. "Spiritualisme," *Œuvres*, 2:221; Appendix D—Spiritualism in *The Philosophy of Jules Lachelier*, 115.

51. Ibid., 2:221/116.

The Living God

1. Lachelier, *Œuvres*, 2:194–95.
2. Ibid., article on "Réalisme," 210–11.
3. Ibid., "Raison," 2:208–10.
4. Ibid., 209–10.
5. "Science et Religion," ibid., 160.
6. Ibid., 160–61.
7. "Notes sur le pari de Pascal," *Œuvres*, 2:48/"Notes on Pascal's Wager," in *The Philosophy of Jules Lachelier*, 104.
8. Ibid., 52/107.
9. Ibid., 52/108.
10. Ibid.
11. Ibid., 54/109.
12. *Oeuvres*, 2:217–18/"Psychology and Metaphysics," 95.
13. Ibid., 218/95.
14. Lachelier, "Pessimisme," *Oeuvres*, 2:203.
15. "La démocratie," *Œuvres*, 2:145, from the meeting of the French Philosophy Society on December 27, 1906.
16. Ibid., 152.
17. "Notes sur le pari de Pascal," *Œuvres*, 2:54/"Notes of Pascal's Wager," 109.
18. Ibid. (Translator's added note.)
19. Ibid., 55/110.
20. Ibid., 56/111.
21. Ibid., 55/109.
22. "Science et Raison," *Œuvres*, 2:165.
23. "Sacrifice," *Œuvres*, 2:214.
24. "Idéalisme," *Œuvres*, 2:189.
25. Ibid.
26. Ibid., 211/"Realism" in *The Philosophy of Jules Lachelier*, 116.
27. Édouard Le Roy, *Le Problème de Dieu* (Paris: L'Artisan du Livre, 1929), 264.
28. Henri Bergson, *The Two Sources of Morality and Religion*, trans. R. Ashley Audra and Cloudesley Brereton with the assistance of W. Horsfall Carter (Notre Dame, IN: University of Notre Dame Press, 1977), 255.

Introduction to Part II

1. Fragment 24, *Écrits de Jules Lagneau, réunis par les soins des ses disciples* (Paris: Union pour la Vérité, 1924), 305.
2. Fragment 13, 301.
3. Fragment 21, 304.

I. Awakening Thought

1. Jules Lagneau, *Célèbres leçons de Jules Lagneau: Évidence et certitude. La perception. Le jugement* (Nîmes: Imprimerie Coopérative La Laborieuse, 1926), 70–71.
2. Ibid., 79.
3. Ibid., 77.
4. Ibid., 79.
5. Ibid., 89.
6. Ibid., 98.
7. Ibid.
8. Ibid., 100.
9. Ibid.
10. Ibid., 114.
11. Jules Lagneau, "Cours sur le Jugement," *Célèbres leçons de Jules Lagneau*, 171.
12. Ibid., 174.
13. Ibid., 175.
14. Ibid.
15. Ibid., 176.
16. Jules Lagneau, *De l'existence de Dieu* (Paris: Félix Alcan, 1925), 49.
17. Fragment 88, *Écrits de Jules Lagneau*, 362.
18. Lagneau, *De l'existence de Dieu*, 58.
19. Ibid., 61.
20. Ibid., 50.
21. Alain, *Souvenirs concernant Jules Lagneau* (Paris: Gallimard, 1925). (Page 81—translator's addition.)
22. *De l'existence de Dieu*, 59.
23. Ibid., 67.
24. Ibid., 61.
25. Ibid., 62 and 72.
26. Ibid., 68.
27. Ibid., 64–65.
28. Ibid., 68.
29. Ibid., 69.
30. Ibid., 51.
31. Ibid., 52.
32. Alain, *Souvenirs concernant Jules Lagneau* (Paris: Gallimard, 1925), 99 (note added).
33. Ibid., 100 (page number added).
34. *Leçon sur le jugement*, 207.
35. Ibid., 203.
36. Fragment 60, *Écrits de Jules Lagneau*, 326.
37. *Leçons sur le jugement*, 224.
38. Ibid., 227.

39. Ibid., 223.
40. *De l'existence de Dieu*, 128–29.
41. Ibid., 129.
42. Ibid., 127.
43. Ibid., 129.
44. Édouard Le Roy, *Le Problème de Dieu* (Paris: L'Artisan du livre, 1929), 216.
45. *Leçon sur le Jugement*, 224.
46. *De l'existence de Dieu*, 147.
47. Ibid., 129.
48. Ibid., 152.
49. Ibid., 148.

II. The Conditions of Certainty: The Monism of Thought

1. Jules Lagneau, *De l'existence de Dieu*, 70.
2. Ibid., 79.
3. "Leçons sur le jugement," *Célèbres leçons de Jules Lagneau*, 173–74.
4. *De l'existence de Dieu*, 83.
5. Ibid.
6. Jules Lagneau, *Leçons sur le jugement*, 212.
7. Ibid., 218.
8. Jules Lagneau, "Leçons sure la perception," *Célèbres leçons: de Jules Lagneau*, 165.
9. *Leçons sur le jugement*, 229.
10. Ibid., 230.
11. De l'existence de Dieu, 88–91.
12. Ibid., 92.
13. Ibid., 81.
14. Ibid., 92.
15. Ibid.
16. Ibid., 80.
17. Ibid., 81.
18. Ibid., 83.
19. Ibid., 81.
20. Ibid., 82.
21. Jacques Rivière, *À la trace de Dieu* (Paris: Gallimard, 1925), 41.
22. Jules Lagneau, *De l'existence de Dieu*, 134.
23. Fragment 4, *Écrits de Jules Lagneau* (Paris: Union pour la Vérité, 1925), 297.
24. Fragment 6, ibid., 297.
25. Jules Lagneau, *De l'existence de Dieu*, 94.
26. Ibid.
27. Ibid., 88 and 89.
28. Ibid., 89.

29. Ibid., 106.
30. Ibid., 105.
31. Ibid., 106.
32. Ibid.

III. Certainty and Action
1. Jules Lagneau, *De l'existence de Dieu*, 60.
2. Ibid., 61.
3. Ibid., 22.
4. Ibid., 23.
5. Ibid., 45.
6. Ibid., 30.
7. Ibid., 31. [Ricoeur abbreviates the cited passage. Lagneau's text says: "the fault in Kant's proof . . . is to have made existence a fact that must be reached outside thought by a belief that is not presented as a moment, a natural degree of action through which this thought posits God in this thought. . . . Kant does not demonstrate God in the act through which the reality of the absolute is posited."—editor's note.]
8. Ibid., 32–33.
9. Ibid., 43.
10. "Leçons sur le jugement," *Célèbres leçons de Jules Lagneau*, 173–74.
11. *De l'existence de Dieu*, 54.
12. Ibid., 129.
13. Ibid., 129 and 132.
14. Ibid., 141.
15. "Fragment 600," *Écrits de Jules Lagneau*, 297.
16. *De l'existence de Dieu*, 74.
17. Ibid., 76.
18. Ibid. Here we rediscover the notion of a symbol that is dear to Lachelier. A necessary duty is a projection, the symbol of our moral act as a free act.
19. Ibid., 57.
20. Ibid., 71.
21. Ibid., 16.
22. Ibid., 78.
23. Ibid.
24. Ibid., 87.
25. Ibid., 88.
26. Ibid., 90.
27. Ibid.
28. Ibid., 91.
29. Ibid., 89.
30. Ibid., 87.
31. Ibid., 86.
32. Ibid., 96.

33. Ibid., 91.
34. Ibid., 96.
35. Ibid., 100.
36. Ibid., 94.
37. Ibid., 86.
38. Ibid., 152.
39. Ibid., 103.
40. Ibid., 102.
41. Ibid.
42. Ibid., 96.
43. Ibid., 97. Here, as in some other passages in Ricoeur's thesis, the word *love* is written with a capital *L*. We have respected this, even for those quotations from Lagneau which do not have the capital letter in the original passages quoted.—Editor.
44. Ibid.
45. Ibid., 98–100.
46. Ibid., 109.
47. Ibid., 100.
48. My emphasis.
49. Ibid., 111.
50. Psalm 42:1 NSRV (New Standard Revised Version).
51. Ibid., 100.
52. Ibid., 152.

Conclusion: The Method of Immanence and the Doctrine of Immanence

1. Maurice Blondel, "Le point de départ de la recherche philosophique," *Annales de philosophie chrétienne* (Juin 1906): 241; "The Starting Point of Philosophical Research," in *The Idealist Illusion and Other Essays*, trans. Fiachra Long (Dordrecht: Kluwer, 2000), 139.
2. Maurice Blondel, "Immanence," *Dictionnaire philosophique*, 344.
3. Jules Lachelier, "Panthéisme," *Œuvres*, t. II, 201.
4. Maurice Blondel, "Le point de départ de la recherche philosophique," 234–35; "The Starting Point of Philosophy," 135.

Index

Alain (pseudonym of Émile-Auguste Chartier), 81, 84
Amiel, Henri-Fredric, 4
Aristotle, 58, 67

Basch, Victor, 64
Baruzi, Jean, xiv, 33
Belot, Gustave, 53
Bergson, Henri 2, 3, 6, 22, 26, 69
Blondel, Maurice, 3, 5, 7, 65, 65, 97, 119, 123, 127, 128
Bossuet, Jacques Bénigne, 25, 50
Boutroux, Émile, 17, 30, 34, 37, 55, 60, 65
Brunschvicg, Léon, 1, 5. 9, 12, 56, 69

Caro, Elme, 30
Cousin, Victor, 19, 26, 30, 38, 39, 53

Dalbiez, Roland, xiv
Darwin, Charles, 30
Descartes, René, 34, 45, 83, 84
Dionysius the Areopagite, 33
Duariac, Lionel, 17
Durkheim, Émile, 5

Espinas, Alfred, 5, 23, 28, 30, 31

Fichte, Johann Gottlieb, xv

Gouhier, Henri. xv

Hegel, G. W. F., 68
Heidegger, Martin, xiii
Hume, David, 3, 38, 39

Janet, Paul, 2, 15, 25, 36, 41, 50, 67, 90
Janet, Pierre, 40
Jaspers, Karl, xvi
Jaurès. Jean, 25, 33, 37

Kant, Emmanuel, 2, 6, 15, 17, 18, 23, 26, 29, 30, 32, 33, 34, 35, 36, 43, 46, 59, 60, 62, 63, 67, 78, 79, 81, 90, 105, 110

Lavelle, Louis, 91
Leibniz, Gottfried, 23, 25, 29, 33, 49, 59
Le Roy, Édouard, 3, 25, 55, 68, 115

Maine de Biran, 19, 26, 37, 76
Malebranche, Nicolas, 128
Marcel, Gabriel
Montaigne, Michel de, 86
Moses, 30
Mounier, Emmanuel, xviii

141

Nabert, Jean, xix

Parmenides, 97
Pascal, Blaise, 61, 63, 65, 110
Plotinus, 69
Plato, 6, 7, 23, 42, 67
Proust, Marcel, 4

Rauh, Frédéric, 5, 25, 35, 39, 42, 43, 55, 63, 67
Ravaisson, Felix, 2, 31, 32, 56, 28, 59, 66
Ribot, Théodule, 2
Rivière, Jacques, 98

Saint John of the Cross, 33, 86
Schopenhauer, Arthur, 7, 63, 64
Séailles, Gabriel, 63, 64
Spinoza, Baruch, 11, 53, 73, 79, 81, 117

Taine, Hyppolite, 40
Thouverez, Émile, 63

Valéry, Paul, 40

Weber, Max 8
Winter, Maximilien, 56

About the Authors

Paul Ricoeur is one of the most important twentieth-century French philosophers, who taught both in France and in the United States. He was the author of many books, including *The Voluntary and the Involuntary, Fallible Man, The Symbolism of Evil, Freud and Philosophy, The Rule of Metaphor, Time and Narrative, Oneself as Another, Memory History, Forgetting*, and *The Course of Recognition*, as well as many essays, including ones on the philosophy of religion.

David Pellauer is professor emeritus of philosophy at DePaul University. He is the author of *Paul Ricoeur: A Guide for the Perplexed* and other essays on the work of Paul Ricoeur. He has also translated or co-translated many books and essays by Paul Ricoeur. He currently serves as a corresponding member on the Comité scientifique of the Ricoeur Archive in Paris.

Perspectives in Continental Philosophy
John D. Caputo, series editor

Recent titles:

Jacob Benjamins, *The Play of Goodness*
Dimitris Vardoulakis, *The Ruse of Techne: Heidegger's Magical Materialism.*
George Pattison, *A Philosophy of Prayer: Nothingness Language, and Hope.*
Irving Goh, ed., *Jean-Luc Nancy among the Philosophers.*
Neal DeRoo, *The Political Logic of Experience: Expression in Phenomenology.*
John D. Caputo, *Radical Theology: Expositions, Explorations, Exhortations.*
Michael Naas, *Class Acts: Derrida on the Public Stage.*
Adam Kotsko, *What is Theology? Christian Thought and Contemporary Life.*
Galen A. Johnson, Mauro Carbone, and Emmanuel de Saint Aubert, *Merleau-Ponty's Poetics: Figurations of Literature and Philosophy*
Ole Jakob Løland, *Pauline Ugliness: Jacob Taubes and the Turn to Paul.*
Marc Crépon, *Murderous Consent: On the Accommodation of Violent Death.* Translated by Michael Loriaux and Jacob Levi, Foreword by James Martel
Emmanuel Falque, *The Guide to Gethsemane: Anxiety, Suffering, and Death.* Translated by George Hughes.
Emmanuel Alloa, *Resistance of the Sensible World: An Introduction to Merleau-Ponty.* Translated by Jane Marie Todd. Foreword by Renaud Barbaras.
Françoise Dastur, *Questions of Phenomenology: Language, Alterity, Temporality, Finitude.* Translated by Robert Vallier.
Jean-Luc Marion, *Believing in Order to See: On the Rationality of Revelation and the Irrationality of Some Believers.* Translated by Christina M. Gschwandtner.
Adam Y. Wells, ed., *Phenomenologies of Scripture.*
An Yountae, *The Decolonial Abyss: Mysticism and Cosmopolitics from the Ruins.*

Jean Wahl, *Transcendence and the Concrete: Selected Writings*. Edited and with an Introduction by Alan D. Schrift and Ian Alexander Moore.

Colby Dickinson, *Words Fail: Theology, Poetry, and the Challenge of Representation*.

Emmanuel Falque, *The Wedding Feast of the Lamb: Eros, the Body, and the Eucharist*. Translated by George Hughes.

Emmanuel Falque, *Crossing the Rubicon: The Borderlands of Philosophy and Theology*. Translated by Reuben Shank. Introduction by Matthew Farley.

Colby Dickinson and Stéphane Symons (eds.), *Walter Benjamin and Theology*.

Don Ihde, *Husserl's Missing Technologies*.

William S. Allen, *Aesthetics of Negativity: Blanchot, Adorno, and Autonomy*.

Jeremy Biles and Kent L. Brintnall, eds., *Georges Bataille and the Study of Religion*.

Tarek R. Dika and W. Chris Hackett, *Quiet Powers of the Possible: Interviews in Contemporary French Phenomenology*. Foreword by Richard Kearney.

Richard Kearney and Brian Treanor, eds., *Carnal Hermeneutics*.

A complete list of titles is available at http://fordhampress.com.

www.ingramcontent.com/pod-product-compliance
Lightning Source LLC
Chambersburg PA
CBHW020415080526
44584CB00014B/1346